Henry Crowder's Memoir
of His Affair with Nancy Cunard
1928-1935

As Wonderful As All That?

by Henry Crowder
(with the assistance of Hugo Speck)

Introduction and Epilogue
by Robert L. Allen

WILD TREES PRESS

Published by
Wild Trees Press
P.O. Box 378
Navarro, California 95463

ISBN 0-931125-05-7

Library of Congress Catalog Card: 87-50416

Cover photo: Nancy Cunard and Henry Crowder at the Hours Press. She
              is operating the ancient press and he is setting type.
              Photo courtesy Hugh Ford

Cover and book design by Nancy Austin

Typeset by Archetype, Berkeley, California

Printed and bound by Edwards Brothers,
Ann Arbor, Michigan

10 9 8 7 6 5 4 3 2 1

PUBLISHER'S ACKNOWLEDGMENT

Special thanks are extended to Ernest Speck, Anne Chisholm and Hugh Ford for their encouragement and assistance in this project.

A Note on Editing

The text published here is the full text of the manuscript written by Henry Crowder and Hugo Speck, with only minor editing. However, the title of the book and the chapter headings were selected by the editor.

R.L.A.

Contents

INTRODUCTION

Introduction

by Robert L. Allen

I F EVER THE PROPOSITION that opposites attract were in need of demonstration one need look no further than the relationship between Nancy Cunard and Henry Crowder. Two individuals with more disparate backgrounds and characters could hardly be found: She the privileged only child, the wildly bohemian daughter of English landed gentry, great-granddaughter of the founder of a famous shipping line; he the youngest of twelve children, the cautiously conservative son of a hard-pressed but pious black family in rural Georgia.

Nancy and Henry were well aware of the disparities in their backgrounds and temperaments, and they found these differences captivating. To Nancy he was "a man who introduced a whole world to me in 1928 . . . A most wary and prudent man, among many other beauties and qualities, who often said: 'Opinion reserved!' Whereas to me, nothing—nor opinion nor emotion nor love nor hate—could be 'reserved' for one instant on the score of things this Man-Continent-People gradually revealed to me about his race and the life of his race." To Henry she "was to open up new avenues of thought for me and because of her I was to change my ideas of life . . . I could not help but notice the intense though impressive eagerness of her attitude. She was no ordinary person. Everything about her down to the smallest mannerisms demonstrated high breeding and graciousness." Nancy possessed "something that I had never discovered in any other person. I greatly admired her intelligence, experience and certain independence of thought."

The relationship was pivotal for both of them—and it culminated in a remarkable offspring, the publication of the monumental anthology *Negro,* an impressive survey of black achievement, which Nancy edited and dedicated to Henry. Nevertheless, when things ended between them, Henry felt disillusioned and embittered.

In 1935–36 when Crowder wrote his account, Nancy Cunard was an internationally famous (racists would say infamous) figure. As a poet and publisher, a socialist and staunch anti-racist, and later as a journalist who would write from Spain during its civil war, Nancy was controversial both for her political views and her personal lifestyle. A bohemian who became a political radical, she was the subject of front page news and back page gossip. Today she is less well known, although a recent biography by Anne Chisholm and the publication in 1970 of an abridged edition of *Negro* prepared by Hugh Ford have again brought her to public attention. Modern readers may require an introduction to her. Much of what follows is based on the work of Chisholm and Ford.

Born in 1896 to Sir Bache Cunard, grandson of the founder of the Cunard line, and the former Maud Alice Burke, a socialite from San Francisco, Nancy spent her girlhood at Nevill Holt, a huge old stone house in the Leicestershire countryside. On the surface it appeared to be an idyllic life. Coddled by nursemaids and governesses, her life consisted of lessons, riding her pony, children's parties, and long walks in the manicured gardens of the estate with her "first friend," the Irish novelist George Moore. When she was older she was taken on visits to museums and the opera in London, and travelled to France and Italy with her parents.

Yet it was a lonely life, and fostered resentments that later flared into open rebellion. Nancy felt unloved and rejected. Though she loved her father he was silent and distant, preferring to spend his time with his horses and hounds or tinkering with metalwork in his shop. A country gentleman, he had no interest in the family shipping business, did not understand his wife, and was puzzled by his daughter. As for Lady Cunard, her view of motherhood was that it was "a low thing—the lowest." The daughter of a socially ambitious mother, Maud Burke rather precipitously married Bache Cunard after having been humiliatingly rejected by a Polish prince whom she hoped to wed. She had earlier had an affair with Goerge Moore while visiting London; Moore remained devoted to her for the rest of his life. Sir Bache, like George Moore, was old enough to be her father. The differences between Sir Bache and Lady Cunard soon manifested themselves. He kept doggedly to his sporting interests while she launched her career as a society hostess, organizing dinner parties, teas and other entertainments at Nevill Holt that brought her into contact with the artistic, intellectual and social elites of London. Nancy was shuffled off to servants so as not to interfere with her parents' lives.

Nancy's one real friend during this period was George Moore who, resigned to having lost Maud, transferred his affection to Nancy. Years afterward Nancy fondly remembered their pleasant garden walks and animated discussions of literature. A deep bond developed between them with sometimes paternal, sometimes erotic overtones. Indeed, it was rumored that Moore was Nancy's father, a rumor he rather wistfully denied when she eventually questioned him about it.

In 1911 Lady Cunard left Sir Bache and Nevill Holt and took Nancy with her to London. She had fallen in love with a younger man, Thomas Beecham, the conductor. For the next thirty years she would devote herself to Beecham and his career as he rose to become a celebrated figure among English musicians.

The departure from Nevill Holt confused Nancy. Leaving her childhood home and her father were upsetting. Moreover, this may have been the point at which she concluded that her mother's social ambitions were paramount,

Henry Crowder. Photo courtesy Anne Chisholm.

finding in men the means for achieving social recognition and leaving little or no time for Nancy.

Nancy responded by developing a spirit of independence that was not always to her mother's liking. She cultivated a group of friends—the Corrupt Coterie they called themselves—who engaged in such daring adventures as all-night masquerades, secret assignations, moonlight swims, and the

Nancy Cunard with African bracelets. Photo courtesy Anne Chisholm.

writing of romantic verses. To her friends she began referring to her mother as "Her Ladyship." The edge in her voice was not lost on them.

As Europe stumbled into the disaster that was to be known as World War I, Nancy began publishing poetry. Six poems appeared in an anthology in 1916, and in the early 1920s she was to publish three volumes of her poems. Her writing was encouraged by the ever-supportive George Moore, and brought her into contact with avant-garde literary and artistic circles.

In a move that surprised several of her friends, Nancy in 1916 married Sydney Fairburn, a young officer who had been wounded in the war. Like her mother before her, Nancy married a rather conventional man who shared few of her interests. The marriage lasted only twenty months and Nancy would later remember it as one of the unhappiest times in her life. But she was anxious to get away from her mother and marriage seemed a convenient way out.

With both the war and her marriage over, and supported by an allowance from her mother, Nancy moved to Paris. Writing poetry and enjoying the cafe life in Montparnasse, she drifted into the unconventional lifestyle associated with the artists and writers of Left Bank Paris in the 1920s. She soon became a well-known figure in her own right. She was attracted to the work of the Dadaists and surrealists, and had an affair with the writer Louis Arragon that ended with him attempting to commit suicide. She became friends with Ezra Pound and Janet Flanner, was photographed by Man Ray and Cecil Beaton, was painted by Kokoschka, John Banting and Wyndham Lewis, and was scultpured by Brancusi. Michael Arlen and Aldous Huxley modelled leading characters in their novels on her. (She also had affairs with both writers.)

Nancy had finally succeeded in escaping from her mother (though still bound to her financially) and she enjoyed her reign in Paris as an unconventional and free-living woman. She achieved a certain notoriety through her appearances in the works of writers like Arlen and Huxley, and she hoped to gain recognition as a poet. The life of a literary bohemian was her first tentative step toward radicalism.

Sir Bache died in 1925 and with the money he left her she decided to buy an old farmhouse in the village of La Chapelle-Réanville, about sixty miles from Paris. This rustic house would serve as her base until World War II, but full of energy and always in motion she was often away from it.

It was through her contact with surrealists that Nancy was introduced to elements of African and black American culture. French surrealists were strongly influenced by African and Oceanic art, and Nancy was intrigued by the masks, fetishes and ivory bracelets available in shops frequented by sailors. She soon began wearing African ivory bracelets, sometimes covering both arms like protective armor. Over subsequent years she amassed an outstanding collection of bracelets. In the cafes favored by her avant-garde friends she also heard black jazz music for the first time. She loved it. She wrote enthusiastically to friends of the new music and her first encounters with performers like the sensational Josephine Baker. As she travelled she made a point of seeking out clubs that featured black music.

Writing years later Nancy would invest her interest in African bracelets and jazz music with a profound psychological meaning. In an autobiographical passage in a book she wrote about Norman Douglas in 1954 she recalled childhood dreams.

> About six years old, my thoughts began to be drawn towards Africa. . . . Surely I was being taught as much about El Dorado and the North Pole? Later came extraordinary dreams about black Africa—'The Dark Continent'—with Africans dancing and drumming around me, and I one of them, though still white, knowing, mysteriously enough, how to dance in their own manner. Everything was full of movement in these dreams; it was that which enabled me to escape in the end, going further, even further! And all of it was a mixture of apprehension that sometimes turned into joy, and even rapture.

Clearly this passage, whether taken at face value as a recollection of childhood dreams or understood as a projection into the past of present feelings, expresses a powerful identification with Africans. On other occasions Nancy spoke of being the "mother" of a black man she had befriended, and she described her "African part" as "my ego, my soul." Hugh

Ford, who worked closely with Nancy in the last years of her life, thinks that she, as a lonely and barely tolerated child, may have felt a spontaneous affinity with a suppressed and rejected race. Whatever the merits of Ford's theory, Nancy was hardly at the periphery of the dance in her dreams and in real life she was to have more than one black man dance around her.

In the summer of 1928, while in Venice with her cousins Edward and Victor, Nancy sometimes visited the Hotel Luna for supper and dancing. Entertainment was being provided by a group of four black musicians billed as "Eddie South's Alabamians." Nancy was thrilled by the group's style, which was new to her and better than the music she had heard in Paris. One evening the musicians were invited to join her and her party at their table. "The charm, beauty, and elegance of these people," she wrote later, "their art, their manners, the way they talked with us . . . Enchanting people, all four, whom we went to hear again and again and often talked with." The pianist in the group was Henry Crowder, whose "great good looks" caught Nancy's eye. The two of them soon became romantically involved and later returned to Paris together.

This was a turning point in both their lives. Crowder was about 33 years old at the time (Nancy gives his birth year as 1895) and she a year younger. Both had been struggling to establish artistic careers—he in music, she in literature. Both were wanderers. Both were restless and open to new possibilities. While they were not looking for each other, there was, curiously, a kind of recognition when they met. Nancy in particular felt that her interest in black culture had now "materialized in the personality" of Henry Crowder.

She invited him to work with her at Chapelle-Réanville where she planned to launch a publishing venture, the Hours Press. Her own third book of poetry, *Parallax,* was published by Leonard and Virginia Woolf's Hogarth Press in 1925, and Nancy was acquainted with the private press movement that was flourishing in England and Europe. In starting the Hours

Press she wanted to learn how to print and to publish contemporary poetry. She had acquired an old Mathieu printing press and set it up at Réanville. As a kind of trial effort, she and Louis Aragon earlier printed a six-page report written by Norman Douglas on the pumice stone industry of the Lipari Islands.

With Aragon's departure, Crowder became her publishing associate. He helped her with the press, accounts and billing, correspondence, packing, and the myriad chores of running a small press. When her driver was sacked, Henry took over as chauffeur. By Christmas they had published George Moore's *Peronnik the Fool,* the "real beginning" of the Hours Press.

Between 1928 and 1931, when it was discontinued, the Hours Press published twenty-four works, both by established authors and relative unknowns. It produced more books than any other small press for a comparable period. The books printed were generally only 10 to 60 pages in length, and print runs were seldom more than 300 copies, but the achievement was significant. Among those published were famous poets like Ezra Pound, Roy Campbell and Robert Graves, as well as newer writers like Walter Lowenfels; Harold Acton, Laura Riding and Brian Howard. Samuel Beckett was "discovered" when the Hours Press sponsored a poetry competition.

Listening to Henry improvise on the piano at Réanville, Nancy was inspired to suggest they publish a book of his compositions. At first he was hesitant, but then he agreed to write the music if suitable lyrics and poems could be found. Samuel Beckett, Richard Aldington, Harold Acton and Walter Lowenfels offered Crowder the opportunity to choose from among their poems any that he might like to set to music. The result was *Henry-Music,* a 20-page collection of music and lyrics (including a "Blues" written by Nancy) published in 1930. It was one of the first times that verse had been set to a jazz score. On the cover is a photomontage by Man Ray showing Henry wearing a hat and coat. Resting on his shoulders are arms (Nancy's, but she is unseen) draped with African bracelets.

Not surprisingly, Nancy's relationship with Crowder precipitated a break with Lady Cunard. Nancy and Henry had lived together openly for more than two years and even visited England together at least twice, managing to keep their relationship hidden from Lady Cunard. Others, however, knew. At a luncheon party in December 1930 Margot Asquith taunted Lady Cunard with the greeting, "Well, Maud, what's Nancy up to now? Is it drink, drugs, or niggers?" Maud Cunard fell into a hysterical rage which prompted Thomas Beecham to send a telegram to Nancy warning her not to come to London. To Maud, Beecham recommended that Nancy be "tarred and feathered." Nancy, never one to avoid a confrontation, left for London with Crowder the same day she received Beecham's telegram.

Nancy was infuriated by her mother's prejudice and hypocrisy, but she could only rail against her in private (and later in public). Maud's power was more palpable. Detectives came by the hotel where Nancy and Henry were staying and its proprietor received frightening messages, prompting them to move to relieve his anxiety. Nancy was afraid that Maud might somehow have Henry deported. He was not, but in a blow that injured Nancy's ego as much as her pocketbook, Maud cut her allowance.

Back in Paris Nancy took her revenge by publishing a vitriolic attack on her mother under the title, "Black Man and White Ladyship." She affirmed her "very close" friendship with an unnamed "Negro friend" and thoroughly castigated "Her Ladyship" for her racial prejudices and social pretensions. Crowder was appalled, but wisely steered clear of the fray.

The last line of "Black Man and White Ladyship" asks: "How come, white man, is the rest of the world to be reformed in your dreary and decadent image?" Nancy had a definite answer to that question in mind. The publication of *Negro,* which she and Crowder were already working on, was to be a resounding refutation of the racists, a proclamation of black achievement, and a celebration of black culture. Nancy credited Henry with inspiring her to undertake this major project.

> Henry . . . was a great deal more than a jazz musician; he was a born teacher, I should say, or at least he became that now as he introduced me to the astonishing complexities and agonies of the Negroes in the United States. He became my teacher in all the many questions of color that exist in America and was the primary cause of the compilation . . . of my large *Negro* anthology.

Crowder, however, exasperated with the twists and turns of life with Nancy, had gone to the U.S. for a visit. Shortly after his return to France she persuaded him to go with her to America in the summer of 1931 to collect material for the proposed anthology. She returned to the U.S. again in 1932, this time with John Banting, to continue her work. She met with black intellectuals and writers W.E.B. Du Bois, Walter White, Langston Hughes, Countee Cullen and other potential contributors to *Negro*. The trips were eye-openers for her but also stressful as the American press, learning of her second visit, hounded her about her black lover, falsely identifying him as Paul Robeson. In a brilliant maneuver Nancy turned the tables by calling a press conference to scotch this rumor. Taking the offensive, she used the opportunity to announce her anthology and call attention to the plight of the framed-up Scottsboro Boys. In the Scottsboro case—which became an international *cause celebre*—nine innocent black youths were convicted of raping two white women. Nancy had circulated a petition on their behalf and was raising funds for their legal appeal. The day after the press conference the New York *Daily Mirror* ran a long story under the headline, "Miss Cunard Asks Aid for 9 Doomed Negroes—Scottsboro Case Draws Girl's Help."

After difficulty and delay *Negro* was finally published on February 15, 1934. Dedicated "to Henry Crowder my first Negro friend," it was an enormous book, containing more than 850 pages of text and photographs. It measured twelve inches by ten and a half, and weighed almost eight pounds. It included 250 contributions by 150 authors, most of them black or "coloured." Although more than half the book was devoted to the United States, there were also sections on Africa, Europe, the West Indies and South America. In a foreword Nancy stated that she prepared the book "for the recording of the struggles and achievements, the persecutions and the revolts against them, of the Negro peoples." By now politically radical, she also asserted that "it is Communism alone which throws down the barriers of race as finally it wipes out class distinctions."

Nancy herself contributed several pieces, including a long essay on Harlem that revealed her empathy with the spirit of the people and her shrewd political insight into their oppression. She also wrote an excellent account of the Scottsboro case, and a historical overview of Jamaica in which she also assessed the strengths and weaknesses of Marcus Garvey's black nationalism. Henry wrote a reminiscence, called "Hitting Back," of his experiences, including street fights, with racists in America, and a short essay affirming that in Europe "color prejudice, though it exists in some places such as England, is never, as in America, a religion or creed." The book also contained samples of Henry's music and Nancy's poetry.

In the scope of its subject matter and the variety of its contributors *Negro* was an impressive book. The American section, for example, was subdivided into sections on slavery, patterns of Negro life and expression, Negro history and literature, Negro education and law, accounts of racial injustice, Negroes and communism, the Scottsboro case. There were sections devoted to Negro stars, music, poetry, sculpture and ethnology. The list of contributors included many individuals who were then or have since become well-known: Langston Hughes, Zora Neale Hurston, W.E.B. Du Bois, Theodore Dreiser, William Carlos Williams, Josephine Herbst, Sterling Brown, Countee Cullen, Arna Bontemps,

Ezra Pound, Mike Gold, Alain Locke, Arthur Schomburg, George Padmore, Samuel Beckett, Johnstone (Jomo) Kenyatta, Nicolas Guillen, Jacques Roumain, William Plomer, Walter White, and William Pickens. Raymond Michelet, a young French writer who was actually Nancy's main collaborator on the project, wrote a competent overview of African empires and civilizations, and Edgell Rickword, who assisted in getting the book published, annotated a collection of 18th century slavery documents.

The tenor of the book was militantly anti-racist, but within that there was a range of political viewpoints represented, with some of which Nancy did not agree. In footnotes and comments she occasionally took exception to her contributors' views, as when she excoriated the "bourgeois liberal" politics of Du Bois and the National Association for the Advancement of Colored People. (At the time the NAACP and the Communist Party were battling over control of the Scottsboro case defense.)

Negro was a black manifesto. It cataloged wrongs and abuses and declared that they must cease. It surveyed literary, artistic and intellectual achievements and declared that they were good. It looked the white man in the eye and declared that, in Nancy's words, "the white man is killing Africa." Nothing like it had been published before; nothing like it would be seen again until the black cultural revolution of the 1960s.

Anne Chisholm, Nancy Cunard's biographer, asserts that *Negro* was Nancy's greatest achievement. But the book was the offspring of an intense personal relationship, and Henry Crowder must also share the credit, as Nancy always acknowledged, for its existence. Unfortunately, like too many fathers, Crowder's main contribution was the seed, and by the time of the birth of his offspring he had developed grave doubts about both it and its mother.

AS WONDERFUL AS ALL THAT?

My sincerest thanks to Hugo Speck, an American newspaperman working in Paris, for the helpful suggestions and timely advice he gave me in writing the following pages. The story is mine, told in my own way, but the assistance he gave me in recording that story, I found to be of inestimable aid. I want to thank him publicly.

—HENRY CROWDER

Preface

IT IS OFTEN SAID that every man can tell at least one good story. But whether good or bad the story of my life and what it has brought is told for very definite reasons. I feel I owe it to my race to let it be known what was in my mind during my struggles, and especially during the years one of the strangest relationships that has ever taken place between a black man and a white woman was being unfolded.

A great many people will no doubt consider me a very stupid fool for continuing that peculiar association when I found out where it was leading. They will not understand why I did not quit then and there once the discovery was made. The question also arises for what good reason do I disclose all of the sordid details of this relationship?

To find the reply, the following pages must be read but there is one reason more. As the astounding character of the woman who is mentioned unfolded itself, as I became conscious of the almost dangerous and sometimes harmful nature of her activities, I visualized writing the story.

But don't misunderstand me. In doing so the little financial gain I might receive interests me not at all primarily. It is my hope that the experiences which I have gone through may be of some value to colored men who become enamored with white women.

I planned to write the story at least three or four years ago. I refrained from actually doing it then from personal scruples. I then discussed the proposition with the West Indian writer Eric Waldron in London and told him of my reasons for writing my experiences. He told me that I certainly should do it and offered to assist me. I refused his assistance then. Now I am doing it alone.

Maybe when my background is better understood, when my meager beginning is related, those who now scoff at me for writing such a work will be more tolerant, will say that I have told a story that should be told. I hope so.

CHAPTER I

Up From Georgia

GEORGIA. There in the foothills of the Appalachian mountains in the 1890s a venerable old colored gentleman lived and did his best to father his 12 children. I was the youngest of the 12.

"Brother" Crowder, as he was called by the "brethren" of the Baptist church he so staunchly supported, did the best he could for his kids in the small town of Gainesville where he lived. But being a deacon in the church brought no pay and his other earnings were small.

Fortunately for Brother Crowder he had married a good and thrifty wife. She was more than half Red Indian and not afraid of work. She did what she could to earn money by taking in washing and ironing from the white folks.

We kids all knew what hard times meant. A piece of candy was a rare treat; a whole bag to ourselves an unknown luxury. Yet we managed.

My father was an honest and respected man. By the whites of the village he was considered a "good nigger" and he did everything he could to make his children grow up to be as respected and honest as he.

Before I was old enough to become aware of my surroundings the family moved to the little manufacturing town of Buford, near Atlanta. Leather production was the chief industry of the place so my father and oldest brother worked in the tanneries.

Besides myself there were four brothers and sisters then living at home whom I remember. There were also three grandchildren which made the household consist of 13 people, including my father and mother.

As my father only earned about six dollars a week my mother continued to do her washing in order to help. The earnings of my older brother when he worked—and that was only spasmodically—went mostly to gambling. His name was Paul and we would only see him at intervals. He would disappear when he had earned a little money and would stay away until he had reached the absolute end of his tether. Then he would be off again.

The remainder of us children were raised in a very strict religious atmosphere. My father had been a deacon in the Baptist church when we left Gainesville but he refused to have anything more to do with the Baptists at Buford. He started a small independent Sunday school that was attended by the other colored people of the village who did not like the creeds and beliefs of the Baptists.

I shall always remember those Sunday sessions which my father conducted. I would always stand near him, and gazing up into his face with admiration and pride, sing the hymns he led with energy and all the volume my voice would give.

My father's other religious activities were among the white folks. He kept the white Presbyterian church clean and besides receiving a small allowance for this work he was allowed to sit and listen to the Sunday sermons. He was the only Negro in town granted that privilege.

"And on the seventh day ye shall rest" was interpreted in the strictest manner by my father. Sunday was a sacred day in our house. No activities were allowed but the cooking of meals and the most necessary house cleaning. On Sunday morning we were all bathed and dressed for the Sunday service and no one but mother was allowed to be absent from those meetings.

After the service and Sunday dinner we were not permitted to engage in any sort of games or amusement. Unless we sang hymns to the accompaniment of a small organ we owned we were compelled to keep quiet. Dancing of any form was forbidden at all times. Cursing or swearing was unthought of by any of us and considered to be most wicked in others.

My father was highly respected by both the white and colored people of the town and the family lived proudly in his reflected goodness. My mother, with her Indian blood, always carried herself with a quiet, aristocratic air. She was also deeply religious and always did her utmost to instill the fear of God in us children.

Although I was the baby of the family I received little petting and pampering. I was an emotional child however. In the midst of these religious surroundings I tried to be goodness itself. To even think that I had hurt the feelings of someone would make me miserable in my childish way.

I remember that when hog killing time came in the late fall of the year I would always go into the house and cover my head in the bed-clothes until the ordeal was over. I could not bear to see even a hog have its throat slashed and to witness the ensuing rush of blood always made me sick at my stomach.

I had made a reputation of never telling a lie. I scrupulously tried to live up to this in every respect. When there was a fight or a quarrel among the kids my word was always the final one in deciding the matter when the mothers emerged to settle the dispute. I was indeed a goody good little boy who gloried in hearing his mother tell friends or neighbors what a perfect child was Henry.

On the other hand I don't think there was anything soft about me. I loved all outdoor life and participated in all the activities of the Negro children of the neighborhood. We roamed the woods hunting berries and nuts. We chased rabbits, fished, climbed trees, engaged in rock-battles and occasional fights with the white boys. But I did refrain from doing the more naughty things that are common among young boys. So instilled was I with religion and a fear not only of God but also of the devil that up to my young manhood I lived a singularly clean life.

As the years passed my father became more and more

hopelessly in debt, principally because of the many mouths he had to feed. He had unlimited credit in the stores of the town but could see no possibility of ever getting clear.

How he ever justified the decision I have never been able to understand but early one morning he took the whole family and moved to Atlanta. He evidently felt that his chances of earning money there were better and he knew his younger children would have the chance of a better education.

But he was mistaken about the money. We did get along but were forced to live in squalor and poverty. My father took up carpentering in a small way and my mother became a scrub woman, we needed money so badly. Both my brother James and I were sent to school. I tried to earn some money after school hours by selling papers but I did not earn much at that job.

Paul was still roaming about the country and Noah, another brother, was dead. James and I were the only boys left at home.

When we moved to Atlanta I was immediately sent regularly to a Baptist church by my parents though they were not so energetic about going themselves by that time. They still insisted that I say my prayers each night before going to bed and I did it with regularity and earnestness. I still believed absolutely in the efficacy of my prayers. God and everything pertaining to the Diety had my most profound respect and reverence. The sermons of the preachers moved me to the depth of my being and they still do to this day for that matter. I was almost fanatical in my beliefs and trusts.

I remember how impressed I was at the first service I ever witnessed in a Catholic church. I had great confidence in people and this faith persisted for years until so many bitter experiences made me alter my opinions. Even now though my inclination is to believe a person rather than distrust him.

After I entered school my progress was rapid. I completed a regular eight-year course in five-and-one-half years. I had a good strong voice and used it to advantage. James was also a good singer and quickly learned to play the piano.

Although I believed it wrong to do so, I secretly envied my brother because he could play. That is probably the real reason I learned to play myself. When I used to watch him play for the kids as they marched in and out of the room I secretly vowed I would learn to play also.

The chance to do so came shortly afterwards. I found a job at the colored branch of the Y.M.C.A. I timidly asked my boss if I could use the piano in one of the lounge rooms.

"Can you play?" he asked me.

I timidly hung my head and mumbled:

"A little."

But he consented, so during my free hours I laboriously began learning to play. It was a tedious task but I stuck with it for I wanted people to say I was a better player than my brother. When I was finally rewarded with that compliment I felt I had achieved a great success.

It was also during these latter years I spent in grade school that I had my first opportunity of visiting the north. All my life I had heard of the way Negroes were treated there and it had long been my ambition to see it all for myself.

The chance came because I could sing. A growing industrial school in Atlanta was going to send a quartet of young colored students on a tour through the New England states during the summer. I was selected as a member of the foursome.

In every respect this trip was truly a revelation to me. In the company of another young colored man, who was a student at the school, we travelled northward to meet our manager in New York. This was the first time I had ever left the Southland so it is not hard to imagine some of my feelings once we crossed the Mason-Dixon line.

We travelled in coaches for Negroes as far as Washington. From that city north, as there were no colored coaches on the trains, I had my first contact with white people on anything like an equal basis. As it happened, we entered a coach that contained no black people other than my companion and myself.

The seat we occupied was directly behind one which a

white man had taken. I paid no particularly attention to him until sometime after the city limits had been left behind. He then turned and asked us:

"How does it feel to be riding in the same coach with white people?"

We were slightly startled but as I remember we made no reply. But I do recall having a feeling of resentment at his speaking to us in this manner, and especially at the patronizing tone of his voice. In truth, I did not feel one whit better by being near him. I only felt a certain satisfaction in knowing I could sit anywhere I pleased as long as I had paid for a ticket.

We had no chance of seeing New York when we arrived there for our manager whisked us away to New England to start rehearsals for our tour. This included a number of summer hotels and camps along Lake Champlain and the Adirondack mountains.

This was a new world to me. I was fresh from the dirt and poverty of the alleys of Atlanta. Being suddenly removed from one part of the country where all colored people are "niggers" to a section where the color of my skin seemed to make little difference caused me no little excitement. Every-. where we went we were received cordially as though we were human beings with hearts, souls, likes and dislikes very similar to everyone else.

And because we were black, it pleased me all the more that we made such a success. Besides being the baritone of the quartet I was also the reciter. I could recite entire Negro poems in dialect and the holiday makers seemed to enjoy these, especially the children.

The experience of attending a dance in one town in Massachusetts I shall never forget. I marveled at the manner in which the few Negros present mingled and danced with the whites as if they were one of them. I did nothing but watch for a long time but I finally got up enough courage to ask a white girl to dance with me. She readily consented and I found myself dancing with a white woman for the first time in my life.

After the first few moments of shy hesitancy the strangeness of my position faded and I felt no different than had I been dancing with a girl of my own race.

Long after the dance was over I pondered in my mind why it was that white people thought themselves so much better than the Negroes. Although this question had often been in my mind I have never found an answer which completely satisfies me.

I remember that I got no thrill from the contact with the white girl but thoroughly enjoyed the dance because she happened to be an excellent dancer. I did not seek that girl's company again that evening but I enjoyed myself immensely.

In all, the trip was a big success and when we returned to New York I felt that my ideas about white people would have to be revised. I have revised them radically since but the revision never took place at that time.

During the time we had spent in New England big race riots had occurred in Atlanta. Being constantly on the move, and due to the very meager reports that did reach us, we knew little of the seriousness of the disorders. So I boarded a train for Atlanta feeling in a very different mood toward the whites in general than I possessed when I left the south.

When I arrived at home I emerged from the station to find the city ominously quiet and the streets absolutely deserted. I did not think much of this, however, as the hour was late. I decided to walk home as I only had one bag and not much in that.

I proceeded only a few paces though when a policeman told me I had better take a cab as it was dangerous for "niggers" to be seen on the streets at night alone. I took his advice for I then realized some serious incidents must have occurred during by absence.

Before I reached home, however, my dampened spirits had revived somewhat and I decided to play a joke on my old father. We lived in a shadowy back street that was lined with two-room houses for Negroes in a quarter called "Dark-Town."

I rapped on the door and from within my father asked who was there. I replied very sternly:

"Never mind, open the door!"

I heard a shuffle inside and in a few minutes the key turned in the lock. As the door swung slightly open I saw the muzzle of a murderous-looking pistol in the shaking hands of my father. He again demanded who was there and asked what was wanted.

I quickly made my identity known, thinking all the while what a fool I had been.

As the following day was Sunday I went to a certain street corner opposite a big church that was always crowded with colored people, especially after morning church services. I went there expecting to find a lot of my friends and acquaintances. To my great surprise the corner was deserted.

I then went to the homes of my friends and found them in a state of terror. The graveness of events during the previous week dawned upon me as, one after another, my friends told me what had happened. Scores of Negroes had been ruthlessly killed and many more imprisoned. Their houses had been searched and all weapons found had been confiscated. A cordon of soldiers had been thrown around Dark-Town and no Negro was allowed to either enter or depart from the locality without satisfying the soldiers as to his business. It was reliably reported from several sources that many white people had also lost their lives in the disorders.

I was amazed. All of my pleasant dreams of the past summer went glimmering. All of the old hatreds and distrusts that I had been taught all my life returned with new vigor. I knew that Atlanta and the south would never be the same to me again. I had previously thought that my home was the best place in the world in which to live. Then, I only hoped for the day to come quickly that would be the last for me in Dixie.

During the months that followed I lived through a period of great oppression of Negroes by the whites of my city and state. I learned to hate white people and particularly the

men. I blamed them for terrorizing their women to the point
of making them sacrifice many Negroes' lives in an effort to
maintain the reputed purity of white women.

I never thought them superior. I have always thought I
was as good as anyone and better than a great many. I have
never desired to be on a plane of social equality with anyone
who does not want me there. I don't want to eat at a table
with anyone who does not wish to eat with me. I detest
having a person in a seat beside me anywhere if I have the
slightest suspicion that person does not want me to sit there.
If anyone does not want my company I certainly don't want
theirs.

But the right to enjoy the privileges accorded to every
other person whatever his color, I consider no more than my
just due. People should be allowed to arrange the personal
and private part of their lives to their own liking so long as
it does not interfere with the public good.

So, soon after my return I decided that for myself the
idea of social equality with white people meant nothing to
me. But I did long for the great opportunities they had to
better themselves and thus accomplish great things.

CHAPTER II

Mahogany Hall
and Other Houses

RELIGION, RELIGION—I was completely saturated with it. I don't suppose there was a colored boy in Atlanta at that time who "had more religion" than I. During all the years I was in school I was an ardent member of the church and eagerly took part in all its activities. At one time I was organist, at another an usher and an officer in one or more of the young people's societies.

I read the Bible regularly and was so devoted to the church that it was once proposed I study for the ministry. That plan never materialized and I am glad now it never did.

But fanatically religious as I was I still had my troubles "wid de debil." As with all young boys, early adolescence brought the usual sexual desires. At first I did not attach any special importance to them but the devil with his devious ways did his damnedest to make me recognize and satisfy them.

The boys of my age were engaged in all sorts of shady affairs. They told me about them but my "religin" would not allow me to emulate them. I felt I had God on my side and the devil would never get me. I admit I wanted to do some of the things I was told about but something within me would never give its consent.

I was terribly shy for one thing and I would sooner have stuck my head in a fire than to have made an improper proposal to a girl. The very thought of such a thing would cause me to blush under my black skin. I had very much respect for the decency and the goodness of women and really believed that they were pure. I could not believe some of the stories which were told to me for my experiences with life at that time were in their infancy.

And this reluctance to approach a woman is part of me even to this day. The early teachings I received in life have stuck to the extent that it is impossible for me to say anything improper to a seemingly respectable woman unless she makes the opening. On the other hand I am sorely afraid of a rebuff. Nothing makes me more miserable than to be told that I have spoken out of turn.

But the devil kept after me. He caused me many hours of physical agony which I tried to bear with silent fortitude. I was fighting just as hard as the devil and I did everything possible to gain control over this passion.

I went in for strenuous athletics at the Y.M.C.A. where I worked. I was good in all gymnastics and was the best boxer in the association. I did so well with the latter that I once considered taking up boxing as a profession. But here again my environment, training and natural disposition prevented my doing so. I played baseball and I still have a scar on my face as a momento of a collegiate football game in Atlanta.

Reading also took up a great deal of my time. There was a nondescript library at the Y.M.C.A. of some 200 or 300 books. I must have read practically everthing there. I also kept pounding away at the piano. I was always passionately fond of music but the attitude of my parents and the lack of money prevented me from having a teacher so I struggled along by myself.

It was no easy job however. I was still in high school and the family was still in financial difficulties. James had quit his job and left home so I had to give all the money I could to my mother.

With all of these difficulties though I did manage to attend Atlanta University for one year. But at the end of that time I had to quit and go to work. My first fulltime job was in the post office. I carried letters for a number of months and it looked as though I might save enough to return to the university, but the devil had other ideas.

In fact, the devil's ideas no doubt changed my entire life for he was the cause of my having to leave town.

She was a good-looking high-brown girl. She was my first real love. I respected her; I thought her the sweetest thing a Georgia sun ever shined upon. I was blindly in love and because I was so blind I could not see the trap the devil was setting for my special benefit.

Unknowingly, I walked into "just one of those things" with my eyes wide open. Although the relations I had with the girl were all of the most respectable nature they were not where other colored boys were concerned. "Just one of those things" for me turned out to be an immediate marriage or leave town. Because I knew I was not responsible, I chose the latter.

I explained the entire thing to my father, bade my family and the south farewell.

My first stop was Richmond, Virginia. Two weeks of severe trials and disappointments brought no results, however, so I journeyed on to Washington, D.C., the town I now claim as my home.

In those two anxious weeks I had done a lot of serious thinking. For one thing I resolved that I would never blindly trust another woman. I knew it to be perfect nonsense to think or say I would never fall in love again but I did tell myself that I was going to be much, much more careful in the future.

I knew that I was once and for all upon my own and it was up to me to make the best of the situation. I did not realize then, however, how the years I had spent in Atlanta would influence the remainder of my life.

I arrived in Washington with another colored boy whom I had left Atlanta with. He was ill and was growing progressively worse as the days went by. We were both penniless but found a friend in an old Negro man who ran a lodging house near the slum district. He took us in.

The next day was Sunday and I was awakened by the chimes of a nearby church. The devil may have chased me out of Atlanta but my "religin" stuck. Then and there I said a prayer for food for both of us were very hungry. I still had faith in my prayers so I left the other lad behind and went into the streets.

The air was chilled by approaching winter. I shivered as I walked down one of the big avenues looking for something that might produce food. Fortunately I did not have to walk far. As I passed a restaurant I noticed a man I had known back in Atlanta. He was polishing the brass rails at the entrance of the place. I approached him, told him my story, and asked if he knew of a job anywhere.

He thought for a minute and asked if I could wash dishes. I replied that I would do anything just then in order to fill my stomach. Luckily for me the dishwasher of the place had quit the night before and I was immediately hired.

It is often truly said that cooks and waiters never go hungry. This could also be said of me in that instance. Very shortly after the serving of breakfast had started my stomach was full. By night I had salvaged enough food to take home and relieve the hunger of my companion.

That job lasted just long enough for me to get a room out of the slum area and begin to feel independent again. My boy friend was suffering from a dread social disease and was compelled to go to the hospital for treatment. I never saw him again until years later.

I lost the next job I had because of my love for music. I was butler and handy man for a prominent Washington couple with no children. They had a beautiful piano and great stacks of music. They were so busy with their social affairs that they were little at home. One day as I dusted the music room, enviously eyeing the piano, I became very interested in some of the music. I decided to borrow a number and take it to a dance place I knew of on my evening off and practice the piece. The cook saw me leave with the music and reported me. I was fired on the spot.

Again I returned to the slum district and secured a bed in a room with three other men. I had very little money and wanted to make it last as long as possible. On the very first night there every cent I had was stolen. I was again stranded, without friends or a job.

Luck was still with me here again or maybe it was my prayers because I was still religiously putting great faith in praying. A piano player was needed in the diningroom below. I got the job. As pay I received a bed to sleep in, food and tips. There was no salary attached. But it was mid-winter so I eagerly took the position offered.

But I hated my surroundings. The place was one of the lowest dives in that part of town. I was in the midst of gamblers, pimps and loose women of the worst type. I had to swallow my religion for the moment or go hungry but I planned to get out as soon as possible. I longed to be with respectable people again for I had not forgotten my early training.

Despite my low companions throughout the week I still attended the Sunday afternoon Y.M.C.A. meetings and was soon playing the piano for the services. Bitter irony that— ragtime tunes for the whores and their lovers during the week but holy hymns for the religious on Sunday. I tried to forget my weektime job for I wanted to get back into the church and mingle with righteous people but fate directed otherwise.

I played the only card I had in the hole but it was not an ace—I knew a man high in the councils of the Y.M.C.A. I told him of my plight and asked him if he could render a little financial assistance so I could change my mode of living. I only asked for a paltry sum he could well afford. I promised to repay him in a few days but he turned me down flat. In addition he gave me a lecture on the mistake I had made in leaving home.

This man had known me for some years and knew that my life had been of an exemplary nature. But all my pleadings of wanting to get away from the dangers of the district were of no avail. He flatly refused me.

That man instilled the first thoughts in my mind as to the hypocrisy of religion. As I left him I began to have doubts as to the good that being religious did anyone. Here was an example of a man with money who professed to be religious. Yet he flatly refused to help an equally religious man who was in peril of falling deeper into the clutches of the devil.

"Well," I reasoned to myself, "if that is real religion then I am going to look out for myself and religion can do the same." I was sadly disillusioned and decided there was no need having any scruples in the matter. From then on I was determined to take care of myself and to hell with the man who got in my way.

I thereupon dropped my religious beliefs cold and accepted the first offer that came my way which promised more money. It was a job playing and singing in a brothel which I obtained through a colored maid who worked in one of the largest and most famous "houses" in Washington.

From a low, dingy hotel restaurant haunted by gamblers and their girls I dropped to a downright whore house. I earned good money, however, bought new clothes and moved into the most respectable neighborhood in town. And all desires to mix with the religious lay dormant. The first experience had "cured me" as far as religion was concerned.

So I continued on my downward path. During the time I had been working in the hotel restaurant I started an affair with the housekeeper of the place. This was of course a colored hotel because Washington, like many towns further south, segregates its races. Negroes are also barred from the white restaurants and hotels in the capital and prohibited absolutely from entering the white theatres.

In the south, Negroes do have a segregated section in all of the large theatres but in Washington they are not allowed this doubtful privilege.

This woman had been very kind to me. Because I was young, I suppose and had left my home, she more or less took pity on me. Her interests at first, I expect, were more of a motherly nature than any other. As time went on, however, an affair developed. Unfortunately for me, she fell in love.

Up to that time the only love affair I had ever experienced had been a heart breaker. It had caused me to leave my home and give up what looked like a promising future. I don't think I have ever really loved any woman since.

When I realized what this woman's feelings were for me I began to seek a pleasant and agreeable way out. I was sorry for her and did not want to hurt her feelings but I did want to get out of it all. I tried but I could not find a possible plan. For the time being the affair was allowed to drift.

By saving my money from my new job I had been able to take a flat, furnish it and buy myself a piano. When I moved from the hotel the woman insisted on coming with me. I was in a mess. I had never dreamed of living with a woman and when brought face to face with the situation I did not know what to do.

She even threatened to kill herself if I did not let her move in with me so I finally consented. I knew well enough that I had made a terrible mistake. Later events proved I was right but at that moment I could find no agreeable way of ending it as I wished.

So the devil and I continued riding together. Often during the four following years I would ask myself if I was going to continue like that forever. Each time the question arose I would tell myself no but still I stayed with my mistress and worked in the brothel.

Entering the place where I worked often reminded me of the great change that had taken place in my life in such a short period. It was a strange experience for me. With all of my religious training, beliefs and thoughts, the work there furnished a marked contrast to all of the things I had been taught to respect and desire.

How well I remember my first introduction to the district and how very timid I was about ringing the bell of the pretentious-looking house to which the little colored maid had sent me. I remember just as well the events that followed.

What a surprise it was to me when a gorgeously gowned and jeweled woman came to the door. Under the soft white and red lights she looked like a white woman but I was too amazed at her striking appearance to be sure.

I told her why I was there and she politely asked me to enter. The floor of the house was covered with a thick, soft carpet. From there I was shown into a magnificently furnished room and told to wait.

It was the first time I had ever been in a house of ill-fame and I was none too comfortable. I took in my surroundings with the greatest surprise and interest. Rich curtains, half concealed by heavy drapes, hung at the windows. The furniture seemed of the best quality and was beautifully upholstered. Two large oil paintings of nude women hung on the wall.

In the midst of my bewildered thoughts a stout mulatto woman, clad only in a yellow silk robe, entered and told me she was the "Madam." We immediately started talking business. I was to report for work at nine o'clock in the evening and play the piano and sing until the house closed in the morning. The pay was two dollars a night and tips. I accepted and was told to come to work the following night.

My mind was in a whirl as I left the house. I had never imagined places of that sort could be so grand.

The following evening I presented myself at the door promptly at nine o'clock. I was startled upon entering, however, by being told that since I was the first man to enter the house that night I would have to hand over a piece of silver money for luck. If I did not have the money I would have to wait until some other man proceeded me and gave a present. Being anxious to get in and get my bearings I surrendered my last dime.

I was shown into the ballroom where I was to play and sing. It was furnished with a lovely piano and a number of chairs. The floor was highly polished and the windows draped in thick red plush. The usual nude pictures hung on the walls.

A number of beautiful mulatto women sitting in the

room eyed me curiously as I entered. They were all dressed in magnificent evening gowns, and their faces powdered and painted as though an expert had applied their make-up.

I was terribly ill at ease. I very shyly took a chair that was near the piano and began to wonder what the start would be like.

This house was the famous Mahogany Hall of Washington, D.C. A lot of southern cities have houses called by the same name but I dare say they are not as magnificent as the original was in those days.

All of the women who worked there were light colored and catered to white men only. As the pianist I was the only black man permitted in the place. I was immediately dubbed "The Professor" and was never called by any other name as long as I was there.

I did not exactly know what to do on my first night there and was beginning to softly play a few tunes when my little colored maid friend who steered me into the job appeared and put me at my ease.

She told me that I need not play except when "company" was there and that it was strictly against the rules of the house to bring whiskey or gin into the house or to flirt with any of the girls. Violation of any of these cardinal rules meant immediate dismissal I was told.

It was not difficult for me to strictly observe these two rules at first but after working there for a while I would smuggle whiskey in for the girls. On those occasions I always received handsome tips.

As time passed I became accustomed to the life of the place and earned good money. The "Madam" and all the girls liked me so I got on very well. The girls had no interest for me personally. I soon discovered that on the whole they were a pretty ignorant, low type. They used filthy language and were generally disgusting when no white men were there.

During the entire two years I worked there I only saw two women who I thought were of a better grade mentally. They both confided to me that they were there only for the purpose of getting some quick money for a special reason. Neither of them stayed long.

The girls were allowed to go out but they had to swear not to associate with colored men. Needless to say that oath was freely violated. In fact I think the only pleasure those girls had was when they were with men of their own race.

The method employed by the Madam to hold her girls was rather crude but it worked. When they entered the house they were bought new gowns for the parlours. The price charged a newcomer was always double what the dress cost. The Madam always paid in cash and the girl would repay for her clothes out of her earnings. Madam always insisted on three dresses to start with and a new one whenever she deemed necessary. The girls received half of the fee charged in the house and out of their pay they had to pay half to Madam for their clothes. The women could never get out of debt.

The police of the district, who were in the pay of the Madam, would uphold her in preventing any girl from leaving if she owed anything. This of course was only terrorism but the girls fell for it although a few did run away in despair and desperation. At best it was a terrible life for them and I felt very sorry for some of them.

The white clients were as a rule very orderly though there were a few brawls and fights started by drunks on Saturday nights.

As I worked there almost two years I came to know all of the other colored men and women of the district. A short time before I started working in the "Division," as the district was called, the police had made the life of the Negro men who worked in the house miserable. They were continually arresting the boys and charging them with vagrancy.

This practice was stopped, however, by a ruling from the police court which said that the playing of a piano in a house of ill-fame did not constitute a violation of the vagrancy law. Thereafter, the piano players were safe.

When I quit my job in the Mahogany Hall I went to

work in the most select house in the district. That house catered only to white men of the highest social and wealthy circles. The girls were all white and wore the most extravagant evening dresses. Needless to say, it was a most expensive house. The only drink sold was champagne and in the event a client desired beer or whiskey it was given free of charge.

Only three men worked in the house. There was a porter and I was assisted by a banjo player. We were all colored. The Madam there would not hire white musicians or maids under any circumstances.

I made more money there than ever before in my life. Sometimes I took home as much as $80 or $90 for a night's work and I never received less than $7.

CHAPTER III

Leader of the Band

THOSE WERE PROSPEROUS DAYS for me but not very happy ones. At first with its newness, its amazing differences from anything I had ever imagined could exist, the red light district held me with a magnetism it is impossible for me to explain.

But as the years passed I became more and more unhappy. True, I was making more money than I had ever made before in my life but the periodic spells of the blues which came over me warned me that I would never be happy if I continued that life.

I longed for something I could not find. Now I know it was my "religin" working from underneath but in those days I could find no definite answer for my desires by the process of introspection.

A beautiful little brown-skinned school girl by the name of Mary Frances Turner eventually provided the answers for me. I had known her years before in Atlanta and met her one evening in Washington where she was attending a girls' school.

Her freshness, her simplicity and her sweetness furnished such a great difference to the women with whom I worked I was immediately attracted to her. Instantly, I started doing everything I could to make this girl like me.

But I had two big stumbling blocks in my way. One was the woman who was still living in my flat and the other was the place where I was working. As the girl belonged to one of the leading colored families in Atlanta that was religious to the nth degree, I knew she would certainly look upon me with contempt should she ever discover my real situation. I certainly did not want her to find out how I was living.

And the longer I went with her the more certain I became that I was willing to give up everything I had and start anew rather than lose her.

In desperation, I decided to act regardless of the consequences. One day I walked out the flat, leaving everything as it had always remained. I refused to go back. I had to endure some terrible scenes with my former mistress but I stuck it out.

I then had only my job in the way. That bothered me considerably but despite that fact I managed to become the girl's constant visitor. She had persuaded me to attend religious services again but my conscience was playing havoc with me concerning my job.

Mary Frances then finished school and returned to Atlanta but a constant correspondence was kept up between us. Being away from her only intensified my willingness to drop everything and start again. I knew I was in love as much as I would ever be. I wanted to marry her.

A little later she attended a big church convention in Philadelphia and stopped in Washington on her way home. The three days she was in the capital were happy ones for me. We were constantly together and before she left we were engaged.

I was determined to throw up my job and find other work as soon as she left but Congress saved me the trouble of at least quitting my job.

The "gentlemen on the hill" had been informed of the "terrible shame this openly protected cesspool of iniquity" shed on the country's capital city. Legislation was rushed through to "wipe the blot" from existence.

In a way I was glad it had happened that way and I immediately began to seek other means of employing my now considerable talent for playing the piano and singing.

I did not have to wait long for soon I found a job with

a small orchestra playing for dinner and dancing in one of the leading restaurants of the city.

Truthfully, I can say that during the entire time I worked among the black and white women in the underworld houses, I never had even a drinking rendezvous with one of them. Although I became more or less accustomed to the life of the district I always tried to hold myself absolutely separate from it.

Again, I was definitely afraid of contact with the girls who worked there. There were many temptations around me but I managed to steer clear of most of them. This is probably due to the fact that when I am working I actually lose sight of my surroundings in a way. I only hear and feel the music and seldom notice the dancers in particular.

Then came the death of my mother. During the years I had lived in Washington I had been back to Atlanta on several occasions. One of these was during the last illness of my father but I was not able to return when he died.

As I neared Atlanta to attend what I knew would be one of the saddest events of my life—the funeral of my mother—I am sure I felt like the most lonesome person in the world.

With the news of her death a great void seemed to come into my life. The woman who had brought me into the world, raised me and done her best to make me an honest man was gone.

I was more miserable than I have ever been in my life. I prayed to God that He forgive me for my sins, that He make me a better man so that I might return to the paths of righteousness and live the life my mother had wanted me to live.

When the funeral was over I felt I could never return to Washington alone. I decided to ask my fiancee to marry me right away and go back with me. She refused, saying she did not see how she could marry at that time.

When she said that I felt as though the whole world had deserted me. I cared for nothing. I only wanted to get out of Atlanta. I was so upset I told the girl I was leaving the next day and never expected to see her again.

I went back to the place where I was staying and packed

my bags. As I was getting ready to leave the telephone rang. It was my fiancee. She had changed her mind and begged that I stay another day so we could get married.

My departure was delayed by 24 hours for the secret ceremony but my wife could not return with me at that time. I left town with no other token of my marriage than a farewell kiss but with an entirely different outlook on life than what I had possessed the day previously.

I was determined to go back and make a success. I was married. I wanted to make a home for my wife and make her proud of me for the things I had done. I wanted to show her that despite my past the future would produce a successful man.

So back to my job with the orchestra playing in the restaurant I went. I studiously applied myself and not many months passed before I became the leader of the band. When that happened I brought my wife to Washington and we started our first household.

With her coming I was the more filled with ambition. My little band became famous and I began to supply colored musicians for parties and dances all over the city.

When I saw I could have bands working for me I took advantage of the opportunity and organized other colored units and booked them under my name. Soon I had seven separate colored orchestras working regularly for me besides the many one night parties and dances for which I supplied musicians.

Happiness in abundance seemed to be coming my way. I had left all of the old regrets of the red light district behind. I was a successful, respected married man who was getting ahead. But I wanted to do bigger things.

I then conceived of the idea of uniting all of the colored musicians in the city in one big organization under my direction. The idea caught on and after some very hard work the thing was accomplished. I became a central figure in the jazz musical field in Washington. I was proud of my accomplishments.

I was doing so well I opened up an office and organized on a big scale. From my humble beginning I felt as though I had more or less conquered the world. No doubt my religious scruples had suffered during these latter years of prosperity. Although I still held the church in great respect and prayed rather fervently I am sure I was placing more dependence on my own efforts than on my prayers.

Next came the war. I did not volunteer for the simple reason that I was a married man. When the first draft came I was placed in the fourth division because I had a wife.

But I did want to do something to help my country. When the "work or fight" plan was organized by the Government I readily applied at the Quartermaster's Headquarters and offered my services as a chauffeur during the day planning to keep my regular job during the evenings.

At first I was assigned to supply trucks but as I was a good driver I was taken off that job and assigned to the White House garage as the Number Two chauffeur of the General Staff.

Luckily or unluckily, as the case may be, I was then assigned to General March. My duties were to drive the General from his home to his office every morning, then to the Army and Navy club for lunch and at the end of the day, drive him home again.

As the shifts were placed, I was subject to his orders for alternate full 24 hours. That meant I worked one day and night but was free the next day and night.

At that time the General had just returned from Europe and I thought rather full of his own importance. He had been received by all of the important persons associated with the Allied Armies in Europe. He was a big man. I was only a black chauffeur.

One day the Cadillac that had been assigned to the General refused to start. It was not my fault for I had nothing to do with the repairs and upkeep of the machine. My only job was to drive it.

So instead of the Cadillac I was given an old Dodge and

told to call for the General and take him home. Dodges in those days had a different gear shift from Cadillacs and the car was new to me.

Nevertheless, I called for the General. He came out of the War Department building very pompously and eyed the Dodge very suspiciously.

"Can you drive that car?" he asked me.

"Yes sir, General," I replied.

He climbed in but I could easily tell he was not pleased. I sensed trouble and was rather nervous.

"Well, go along," he told me when he noticed that I was slowly trying the shift to make sure I was getting it right.

I tried to start but made the wrong shift. Instead of moving off slowly and smoothly, the old Dodge started to jerk and jump.

"What the hell's tha' matter?" the General asked.

"I don't know sir," I meekly replied.

"Don't you know what to do?" he yelled.

"No sir, General, I'm afraid I don't," I replied, beginning to get irritated at his yelling.

In the meantime the car was slowly progressing in great jerks and I was too excited to rectify the trouble.

The General fumed. No doubt he was recalling the high-powered, comfortable cars that had been at his service in France and I was suffering from the comparison.

"Stop the damn thing," he cried, "I won't ride in it another step."

By that time I had lost control of my temper and said: "I don't give a damn if you don't."

"What?" he exploded, "let me out of this wreck."

"Get out General," I replied, "I don't care," for I was practically out of my mind by then.

The General left in a rage and I returned to the garage.

"Where's the General?" the sergeant in charge of the garage asked me. When I told him what had happened he almost fainted.

The General had a brand new Cadillac the next day but

he also had a new chauffeur. No sooner had I parked the
Dodge than I wrote out my resignation. I knew trouble was
coming.

When I handed in my resignation to the sergeant he told
me I could not resign because I was more or less in the army.

"Who says I can't resign," I asked, visualizing all of the
time the trouble the General was going to cause for me.
"Here's my resignation, I'm quitting."

With that I walked out of the place and went home. As
I had volunteered for the service I felt I had a right to resign
but whether I did or not the job was already done. I decided
to wait and see what would happen.

Two days later two policemen called at my office and
informed me they had a warrant for my arrest on a charge of
violating some regulation in regard to my army registration.

I explained my position and was told to immediately
report to my registration board. When I reached there I found
an order had been issued from some source for me to be
immediately certified for service. But I was in number four
class and up to that time class two was just being completed.
I walked out with mixed feelings for I did not know what
quarter to expect trouble from next.

A few days later I received a letter from the Quartermaster's Department notifying me that my resignation had been
accepted but that I could not hold any further Governmental
position during the continuance of the war. I was glad, very
glad.

As the years of the war continued my business continued
to grow. I bought a tailoring shop in the same building where
my office was located and made money on that investment
for a time. For over a year my music and tailoring business
flourished. I made money and spent it fast but I did manage
to make a substantial payment on a large three-story, ten
room house in one of the best sections of the city.

But with the signing of the Armistice in 1919 everything
went wrong for me. People seemed to no longer want musicians and my tailor shop had to be closed. For many months

conditions got worse and worse. Finally, for the first time since I had married I found myself out of a job.

Very little work of any kind was available then. I did find several small jobs but the expense of keeping the house quickly ate up all of my savings. It was one of the worst winters I had ever experienced in Washington.

When spring came I decided to go to Chicago where I had a married sister. From the letters I received from her I thought I would have a better chance of finding work. So leaving my wife behind, I moved westward to a new town and new faces and I hoped new opportunities.

CHAPTER IV

With Eddie South to Paris

I LIKED CHICAGO from the first. I was greatly impressed by the fine way in which the Negroes lived. Although the so-called "Black Invasion" of the far south side of the city was in full swing when I arrived, I marvelled at the freedom the colored folks had in their own section of town.

My sister, with whom I stayed, lived on 53rd Street near Michigan Boulevard and because of the location of the building we momentarily expected it to be bombed by irate whites who thought the Negroes were invading their part of town.

Nothing happened to the building in which she lived but a large, magnificent Jewish Synagogue on Michigan Boulevard less than two blocks away that had been sold to a Negro Baptist congregation was bombed some weeks later. The explosion rocked the entire south side of the city.

But regardless of this new-felt freedom I was still unhappy as I could not find a steady position. Months dragged on without my finding anything permanent so I decided to sell my house in Washington and bring my wife to Chicago.

When she joined me she brought my grand piano and the furniture that had not been sold. With the money that I had received for the sale of the house I bought new furniture and started housekeeping again.

But it did not seem the same. I was happy to have my wife with me again but she evinced a subdued coldness towards me upon her arrival that gave me unpleasant thoughts. I tried to forget them however and kept looking for permanent work.

A job in an orchestra eventually came my way and after

a month or two I organized a band of my own. By dint of hard work I managed to make a first-class band, securing some good contracts. But during a short lull period dissensions broke out among my men. When I discovered I could not get or keep discipline I resigned as director.

After that I found no work for several months. My money was running low. I had been living in an elegant little apartment and studying at the Chicago School of Music. I had also applied for entrance at a leading law school for I had always wanted to study law. All of the plans had to be momentarily dropped.

Small, irritating differences also arose between me and my wife. Whether it was my fault or not I shall never know but it seemed these differences which made life miserable for me always arose between us when I was out of work. Maybe it was because I was foolish enough to believe them, but I began to hear rumors that harassed me terribly. They were the kind that dug in underneath to places where it hurt and it hurt me all the more that I could not track them down.

Luck was still with me however. Eddie South, a well-known jazz violinist, had secured a contract in a big-time nightclub and needed a pianist in a hurry. After some difficulty he located me and there began the trail that led to Europe.

Eddie's band consisted of just four instruments—violin, piano, banjo and drums. Eddie is a real genius on the violin and with every man working in enthusiastic support of his masterly playing the combination quickly rose to fame.

One night Bee Palmer of Ziegfield Follies came to the club and heard us play. She came again and again after the first visit. She created an act with our band as background and we were engaged. I was then in the money again. The Victor people gave us a contract for recording. With my royalties from that work and with my salary I was earning about $250 a week. My bank account was growing rapidly and everything looked rosy again.

Only one small cloud on the sky of our happiness foreboded future trouble. All of my early fears and suspicions in regard to the danger of having any relations with white women that were formed even before I left the Southland began to assert themselves. Eddie, our leader, had seemingly become infatuated with Bee. I sensed trouble.

Eddie at that time was very impressionable and any good looking woman could string him along. In that case he lost his head completely.

One night Bee refused to do her act because a crowded house would not stop talking while she sang. Our contracts for that job were cancelled but we continued at the club and were doing as well as usual. On the other hand Bee decided to go to New York and there our trouble began.

Our Eddie was wild to follow her. I for one was perfectly contented to stay where I was and I have the feeling that the other men aside from Eddie felt as I did. A very trifling argument arose between Eddie and the boss one night. Eddie promptly gave a two week's notice that he was taking his band out of the club.

No amount of persuasion from the manager or the other members of the band could make him change his mind so we were forced to quit the job. Again all of the my plans were jeopardized for Eddie immediately planned to take the entire band to New York. We had done so well and worked up such a fine reputation that no one man in the band ever thought of dropping out of the combination, so we all decided to go to the Big City.

I had five or six hundred dollars saved so I was not worried about the immediate future but I felt very downcast at losing such a good job. At the bottom of my heart I felt it was because this Negro boy had lost his head over a white woman who was not wasting a thought about him.

This proved to be only too true. Eddie left for New York first and we followed shortly afterwards. We naturally went to Harlem. No sooner had we arrived than we immediately scattered. I lived with Eddie in a small apartment and the other boys took rooms in hotels nearby.

The New York venture proved to be a great disappointment. Eddie's affair with Miss Bee was a complete flop. She either could not or would not do a thing for him. We were unable to secure any work despite our fine record. The high cost of living in New York was also eating up the little money I had saved. I decided to close my flat in Chicago and have my wife come to New York. In that way I could at least save the price of maintaining one household.

At last we did secure a job in a small downtown night-club but it only paid about $30 a week. Though it was a terrible drop from our grand position in Chicago we were glad to get it for by this time things had begun to get rather desperate. We worked on there hoping for better things. Miss Bee by that time was only a memory but one that I have recalled many times in my own life and experiences.

With the entrance of a very tall and rather good looking man in the little club one night luck again seemed to be ours. He was accompanied by a very charming and attractive woman whom we later learned was Marian Harris, the singer. He was very attentive to her and we noticed that he seemed to be talking about us. Every time he came he secured a table near the bandstand and often listened to our playing very attentively.

One night he startled us all by coming over and asking us if we would like to go to Europe. I nearly jumped out of my seat. When we learned that he was in earnest we all chorused an affirmative "tickled to death."

Before the week was out we were asked to his house in Greenwich Village where the details were discussed and set-tled. Bowen, as the man was named, was playing sugar daddy to this Broadway star.

He planned on opening a night spot in Paris as tribute of his devotion for her. It was there that she was to shine for his especial benefit. We were to furnish the jazz.

The lady herself seemed loath to go but he was deter-mined and finally succeeded in getting her aboard an Atlantic liner along with us. We had signed contracts giving him our services for a year with an option on an additional year.

In return we were to have all expenses paid while not actually working and some now forgotten percentage of the receipts of the cabaret he planned to open. We all quickly straightened out our affairs in New York and prepared for our trip to Europe. As I had not been able to save any money out of my small salary I was forced to send my wife back to Washington.

Although I was very sorry indeed to leave her behind something told me this parting would mark the end of our ever living together again as man and wife. Never, since I had left Washington had our relations been the same as they were when we were first married.

That "something" it takes to make every marriage a success had been missing since the Chicago days. I had no intentions of deserting her however. I promised to send all the money home I could and did until an absence of news from her led me to believe that she had other interests.

The night I boarded the huge liner that was to carry us across the Atlantic I did not have a cent in my pocket. I had pawned my watch to the banjo player but he had found himself short when he paid his room rent and demanded the money back.

Nevertheless, I was as happy as I could be. I looked joyfully to the future for it promised bigger things than had ever happened in my life. As I philosophized to myself: "At last my chance has come" and I meant to make the most of it.

We were all happy, and as the boat glided down the Hudson and out by the Statue of Liberty, we all shouted for joy. Here was the realization of my fondest dream. It was difficult for me to believe that I was not still dreaming.

And with those happy thoughts came reminiscences of my menial beginning. I could see it all so plainly—my early life, my strict upbringing, how I had strayed from one path to another. But regardless of how far I had strayed from the original road my mother had tried to point to me I still held to the firm resolution that I would have nothing to do with white women while in Europe.

Henry Crowder, late 1920s. Photo courtesy Anne Chisholm.

I had just gone through many lean months because another black man had become infatuated with a white woman. I wanted to gain by this unhappy experience which had compelled me to feel some of its unfortunate results. Yes, I resolved to myself to have nothing to do with white women.

On the other hand there were mingled feelings of going to a new land. Especially were they jubilant for me because of my color. France! The one country above all others I had always wanted to see was only a few days away.

France! No color bar there. No discriminations! Freedom! A chance to live as every other man lived regardless of his color. No taboos. Not a single sigh escaped my being because I was leaving. Only unbounded joy existed.

On their part, the other boys immediately began to plan the good times they were going to have with French women. I could not even think of such things, much less make any plans. I would always say to them:

"You can have all of the fun you want to but I am going to Europe to study, work and save. I care nothing for white women; they mean nothing to me."

They laughed at me and derided what they called my holy intentions. But I really meant it. I was anxious to make good and make something worthwhile of myself.

And this seemed my golden opportunity. A rich man was guaranteeing all expenses for one year, work or no work. I did not intend to let women interfere with my taking full advantage of the marvelous chance it offered.

Fortunately for me the money question was solved on the way across. Eddie and I were in great demand for special parties as entertainers. When we reached Cherbourg I was some 1,500 francs richer because of liberal guests.

The sight of the French coast near Cherbourg gladdened our eyes. There was France at last. How peculiar it seemed. A few days before we were playing in a second rate cabaret in New York. Now we were only a few hours from Paris where opportunity and we hoped success awaited us.

Our first act when we landed was to have a good drink

of Cognac. We next started looking for our manager. After
some difficulty we located the gentleman. He told us to proceed to Paris, giving us the name of a hotel that later proved
to be fictitious. He then disappeared without giving us any
further advice or comfort. We were naturally surprised and
slightly dismayed as he made no effort to help us in any way
for not one of us knew a word of French.

Our troubles were increased by Mike, the banjo player.
He got mixed up with too many whiskeys and Cognacs and
disappeared. We did not know where he had gone and finally
decided he had boarded a train for Paris without a ticket. We
knew if that was so he would be waiting for us when we
arrived there so we took the next train.

It was terribly hot and we were travelling third class but
the joy of being in France made the trip a pleasure. A large
bottle of brandy helped matters a great deal and we were all
feeling pretty good when we arrived in Paris.

We found the banjo player waiting for us on the platform
with a station policeman in attendance. We quickly settled for
his fare and he was immediately released.

A Negro friend who had been notified of our coming
also showed up at the station and directed us to a hotel in
Montmartre. But we went there only after we had vainly
wasted two hours searching for the hotel our manager had
told us about.

The true Parisian auto horn was the first noticeable thing
on our arrival.

As it was dark the city only unfolded itself the following
day but we lost no time in heading for the central point in
Montmartre after getting settled in the hotel.

Before morning we had met many colored friends and
acquaintances we had known previously in either New York
or Chicago. What amazed me as much as anything else was
the number of "The Girls" who were on the streets. I could
not understand how or why they were allowed to solicit
openly without being molested or chased away by the police.
I had heard a lot about them from returning soldiers and

travellers and knew they existed but the reality of the thing was a little more than I liked. But there or not I knew that I was not interested in them in the slightest degree.

I was, however, intensely interested in my general surroundings. I made a careful mental note of everything. I was fully determined from the first to take in everything of that nature which could be gleaned.

Although we were tired and pretty dirty after the ride from Cherbourg one enthusiastic friend insisted on taking us to a "house" and give us our first real glimpse of Paris life.

I went along but saw nothing new. I knew the business—if it might be called that—from beginning to end after my Washington experiences and whether the women wore elegant evening gowns or paraded in nothing they were all there for the same reason. The nudeness of the French spectacle rather disgusted me.

I spent the short time we were there drinking some of the very bad brandy that was served. I have been to these nude bars and houses on several occasions with friends and never yet have I failed to leave without a feeling of repulsion and disgust. I actually shiver when one of those women comes near me. Never do I go there but to oblige some over-excited friend for I personally detest the places. I still think that sort of thing is done in a more refined manner in America.

The few days that followed were ones of great concern for us. We had no idea where to locate our manager who had so strangely abandoned us at Cherbourg. We wondered what had become of him and were uneasy about our future. We were in a strange country without funds with hotel bills steadily mounting. We were in a quandary.

One afternoon shortly afterwards I happened to be walking aimlessly in the Rue Scribe near the Grands Boulevards when I spied a very familiar automobile of an American make parked in the center of the street. On inspection I identified it as the one that our manager had brought over from America with him.

I decided he must be stopping in either of the large hotels

that were on the opposite sides of the street. I hurried back to our hotel and told the rest of the boys of my discovery. We immediately decided to contact both hotels by telephone in an effort to locate our boss.

He was found in the Hotel Scribe. He was very congenial over the phone and asked us to come down to see him. We wasted no time and went straight to his hotel. He gave some varied excuses which meant nothing. We wanted and insisted that he pay our bills and furnish us with pocket money as our contracts called for.

He gave us a little cash and promised to pay our bills and then disappeared again for two weeks. When we next located him he wrote a check to cover our hotel bill which was a large one.

He then told us that the proposition to open the night-club had fallen through and the Broadway star who had come over with him had quickly returned to the United States. Not one single appearance had she made in France.

After he had paid the bills he returned to the United States, leaving us to hustle for ourselves. As we had no money we could neither return to America or hire a lawyer to bring suit so we could collect on our contracts.

When we learned our exact status we began seeking work in earnest. We first obtained a two weeks' engagement at the famous Empire Music Hall. Although this was a new type of work for the band we did fairly well and received a number of offers for work when the time was up.

Among these was an offer to go to Venice for about eight weeks. I was particularly insistent that we take the offer and after considerable discussion it was accepted.

The first visit of ours to Gay Paree was a very pleasant one for me. There were a great many American Negro musicians in town at the time and the night life was gay. Montmartre was much gayer than it is now and the whole town presented a much livelier aspect than it has presented in many years.

The other members of the band went in for Parisian life

with great energy. But I remembered my resolutions. I usually returned early and was up early. I arranged to resume practice on the piano and spent the hours before noon working hard. It had always been my first thought in settling in any place to try and arrange for piano practice. Sometimes this is difficult but I usually manage to get the use of an instrument.

My only contact with a white woman was that of a young French girl who had married a Negro dancer. Their marriage had been a failure. He was in England working and she had come back to Paris. She had returned to the streets where he had first met her when I knew the girl.

She spoke English very well and helped me in many ways but after two weeks I decided the affair had gone far enough. She started talking of my moving in with her and I could not think of doing that. She was the only white woman I made any pretense of knowing the entire time I was in Paris and at no time did our relations become intimate.

So off to Venice we went. Chicago to New York; New York to Paris; Paris to Venice. What would come next? Each move had looked so full of opportunity. Was the trip to Venice going to end as disastrously as the others?

I hoped not. We all hoped not. Somehow I had managed to keep all of my ambitions intact and as the promise for something better presented itself my thoughts turned back to my wife. I found myself planning ahead how I could send her every penny possible and have something saved when I returned to Paris.

CHAPTER V

Breakfast in Venice

I T WAS JUST about twilight on a sweltering mid-summer day in 1928 that the four of us got out of an international train in Venice. The 24 hour trip from Paris had been very trying for the coaches were crowded and we had been forced to stand up for most of the long journey. But there we were in Venice and we were all glad the trip was over.

I remember marveling at the strangeness of it all; the strange faces, strange buildings, strange colors and the pealing of innumerable bells as the sun was giving way to the advancing twilight. I had read about and seen a lot of pictures of Venice but the reality of it was something far beyond my wildest imagination.

After a few brief preliminaries we were all installed in a large luggage gondola and shortly afterwards arrived at the hotel where we were to stay. None of us spoke a word of Italian but we made fluent use of signs to make known our most pressing desires.

First and foremost was a bath. This turned out to be a very intricate and even dangerous process which was never mastered by any of us. This finished, we were escorted to our place of employment which was located next to the Royal Palace near St. Mark's cathedral. It was one of the most fashionable café-restaurants in Venice at the time. There we were informed of the conditions under which we would work and were told we would start the following night.

Venice was a strange and wierd city to me then and to look back over the years it now seems stranger still. Here began a peculiar adventure for me and it is still more peculiar when the circumstances are understood and appreciated.

In due time we started to work, playing to a very aristocratic clientele and immediately achieved success. One evening, on about the fourth or fifth night we worked, we were all startled to see a most peculiar and striking woman enter the ballroom accompanied by a tall man. I say we were startled because Negro musicians always carry on a running fire comment on all women who come into a nightclub, cabaret, or restaurant where they are working.

When this particular woman appeared, looking so thin, so white and so fragile, all sorts of exclamations came from different members of the band and quite a lot of laughter at some of the remarks.

But being true to my promise, I refrained from any comment. In fact, I resented some of the remarks the other boys made about her.

That incident passed but the woman continued coming to the dance night after night. She always seemed to enjoy the music but I don't remember any of us paying any particular attention to her.

Several nights later after the dance had finished, I happened to be the last one of us to leave the bandstand. As I left the ballroom to get my hat I noticed Mike, the banjo player, sitting at a table talking to a man and a woman.

I got my hat and returned to the ballroom to have my night-cap before leaving for the night. I had to pass the table where Mike was sitting with his white friends. As I passed I heard a feminine voice say:

"Won't you sit down and have a drink?"

I stopped and accepted. I then found myself being introduced to Nancy Cunard and her cousin, Edward Cunard. Had I known then what that introduction would bring I would never have stopped. But who is the man who knows where an invitation to have a drink will lead?

With that introduction began my association with Nancy Cunard . . . an internationally known white woman with a

Nancy Cunard, 1930. Photo courtesy Anne Chisholm.

very brilliant mind who speaks four languages fluently and who is a writer and a poetess of note. She is also widely travelled and is well versed in the history of art and painting.

It was she who was to open up new avenues of thought for me and because of her I was to change my ideas of life and opinions about many things.

As I sat talking to her I could not help but notice the intense though impressive eagerness of her attitude. She was no ordinary person. Everything about her even down to small mannerisms demonstrated high breeding and graciousness.

She was not exactly what I would call a beautiful woman but she did make a very striking appearance that compelled attention. I thoroughly enjoyed that first conversation.

The evening ended. We said good night. I returned to my room; went to bed and to sleep. The woman had impressed me as a charming person but not sufficiently to make me want to forget my resolutions or break the regular routine I had set up for myself.

My day in Venice began with a French lesson at the Berlitz Language School. Late each afternoon I put in two or three hours practice at the piano in the ballroom. Then dinner and to work.

It was during one of these afternoon practice periods that Nancy suddenly appeared in the doorway and asked me where the owner of the place could be found. I did not realize until later that this was a strange request to make of me sitting there all alone in the ballroom far removed from any person who could give her the information she sought. Of course I knew nothing about where he might be found so she immediately left without further words.

A day or two later all four members of the band were sitting at dinner when the waiter came and said a lady wanted to speak to the pianist on the telephone. Imagine our surprise and mine most of all for I was not only the most conservative man in the crowd but also the oldest.

All of the other boys had definitely announced that they were on the look-out for the chance to have an affair with some woman of wealth and position. I had always derided their ambitions so we were all naturally startled that I should be the first to get this much-desired opportunity. We all felt that a telephone call from a white woman after such a short time in Venice could not possibly mean anything else. The boys all exchanged knowing glances as I left the table.

Bewildered, I took up the receiver. A very sweet and cultured voice at the other end of the wire asked me to come to dinner. I was agreeably surprised, but as I had actually begun eating I did not know what to say in reply. I somehow stammered out the fact that I had already started my dinner but in a persuasive voice she asked that I stop and finish my dinner with her.

As I stood there and listened to her soft voice coming over the wire my mind was bombarded with thoughts of my oft-repeated resolutions. Was I going to make the first step that may mean the destruction of them all or was I going to "chance" it for this once to see what it would be like?

It was hell. There were the three men behind me who had heard me speak my views on the subject any number of times. There was a soft, persuasive voice in the receiver at my ear dangling an interesting invitation before me. I hesi-tated. . . . I accepted.

"Yes, of course I will come," I heard myself saying.

"Alright," came the reply, "a gondola will call for you immediately."

I returned to the table and told the gang that I was not going to eat anymore; that I had been invited out for dinner. The next ten minutes were both trying and amusing for the boys wasted no words in telling what they thought of my "holy intentions."

Shortly afterwards I was informed that the gondola was waiting. Finished in black and gold and manned by two Ital-ians, it was a stately affair. I was ceremoniously escorted to my seat and we were off. Down the Grand Canal and into what to me were many mysterious and devious turnings.

As the gondola glided noiselessly through the dark wat-

ers, skillfully handled by the two silent gondoliers, my
thoughts were racing. The buildings lining the canals seemed
to possess an ominous, mysterious silence. It all seemed wierd
and unreal. I was frankly perturbed.

Who was this woman, I thought, and what did she want
with me? I began to think of adventuresses and all sorts of
things. I wondered if I was being inveigled into an amazing
European mystery of some sort.

I actually began to wonder if I had not been a fool to
have come and longingly remembered the rest of the gang
quietly enjoying their meal at the hotel while I was being
taken to some unknown place to meet some strange white
woman. I could not for the life of me imagine why she had
invited me.

But I had to see the thing through as I was at the mercy
of the gondoliers. I could not speak a word of Italian and
knew nothing of my exact whereabouts. After what seemed
like hours we arrived and I was shown into a beautifully
furnished Venetian apartment.

Nancy greeted me very cordially and as my time was
short dinner was immediately served.

Of the dinner itself I remember very little. We talked of
a great variety of things but nothing in particular. I found,
however, that I was greatly impressed by the lady's intelligence. I became aware that I was talking to a person of no
ordinary intellect. I somehow felt very small and unknowing
as she said the simplest of things.

After dinner Nancy proposed to show me some trinkets
and treasures which she said might interest me. We moved
into the bedroom which was adjacent to the dining room.
She then showed me some African bracelets, beads and one
or two objects of gold. They were the first of their kind I had
ever seen but in some peculiar manner they elicited my warm-
est admiration. In all, she showed me quite a number of
things, some of which she was wearing.

In the inspection of these articles I often found myself
quite close to her. In fact, at one time our heads were quite

close together. I was non-plussed. I did not know what to
do. I surely did not want to make an ass of myself by presum-
ing to take advantage of what might be just an act of interest
and hospitality.

Yet, and yet. . . !

But I was compelled to reason that her interest in me
was not perfunctory. She was taking pains to be nice to me
and I could not help noticing that the near touching of our
heads at times was not purely accidental.

I realized that I had suddenly become tremendously interested in this lovely woman. She intrigued me in an unde-
scribable fashion. In a few short moments my heart was
thumping at a terrific pace.I could feel my blood excitedly
racing to my head.

But despite this I confined my attention to admiring the
objects. All my shyness would permit was a remark about
the beautiful color of her hair.

We returned to the diningroom and I very reluctantly
told her that I must go. She told me how pleased she was to
have me and that I must surely come again. I replied that I
would certainly be pleased to do so.

I looked at her and what I thought I saw in her face made
me throw caution to the winds. I staked everything on the
interpretation I had made of the glance she had given me. I
forgot who I was, where I was but not what I was doing. To
me, an invitation had been given and I thought it better to
try and fail than not to try at all.

We were standing near the entrance and I was saying
good-bye. We were very close together. I decided to kiss her.
I tried to kiss her on the mouth but she turned her head aside.
The move was wasted.

I felt I had made a blunder and decided on a quick retreat.
As I hesitated momentarily she looked at me quickly and
impulsively kissed me flush on the lips.

Without further action I quickly bid her good-bye and
clambered aboard the gondola. Back to work.

The remainder of the night passed in a haze. My fingers

moved mechanically over the keyboard. I could not for the life of me figure out what it was all about.

The numerous questions of the other members of the band and their teasing and bantering had no effect. I merely smiled and told them no details.

But despite the great pleasure the visit had given and the woman's evident interest in me, I very seriously asked myself where it might lead.

I did not desire any casual affair with any woman at that moment. I had no interest in a flirtation. This lady certainly did not act like a flirt, but that helped me little in trying to solve the problem that had presented itself.

When I went home to bed that night I could not sleep for thinking of the events of the evening. Although my good resolutions were fast becoming a memory they were still putting up a stiff fight for consideration. A battle royal was being waged in my mind.

I became the more perturbed the next day when, after making a few guarded inquiries, I discovered who Nancy Cunard really was. I was continually asking myself:

"Why should she pick me?"

There were the other members of the band: handsome Mike, charming Eddie and vivacious Romie . . . why me?

But despite all of the doubts in my mind the friendship that had started so suspiciously began to ripen. A day or two later after the dance when we were having drinks together Nancy told me that she must go away for a few days to visit Norman Douglas, the British writer, who was then in Florence.

During the days she was away we kept up a daily correspondence by telegraph. In my mind these messages from her removed any last doubts which remained as to what she thought of me but I was still in a turmoil.

To say I was excited would be to put it very mildly. I was longing for her to come back. When she did return I knew the feeling of mutual pleasure was real. When I again saw her I knew that something had happened to me; I knew that the excitement of our relationship, the promises it supposedly held had triumphed. I kept telling myself that I was doing the right thing; that the choice I had made was for the better. But I am afraid real reason had little to do with the decision. I was infatuated beyond all reason.

She shortly came to know all the other members of the band and became quite fond of the drummer's wife, an extremely beautiful colored girl who had travelled from America with us.

The girl proved to be a positive sensation in Venice. Everywhere she went on the streets she was followed by curious crowds. If she stopped to look into a shop window she was immediately surrounded by gaping people. The other boys in the orchestra greatly enjoyed taking her for a walk to St. Mark's Piazza to feed the pigeons because she immediately became the chief attraction there. The painters of the place clamored for her to pose but most of them were too poor to offer any remuneration.

On her side Nancy began giving all of us Venetian glass rings. I received a beautiful one of jade lined with gold. I thought it a very lovely gift.

Many nights after our work was finished she would come to our hotel and interestedly watch the four of us play black-jack or hearts, card games that were new to her. On many occasions she remained until the wee hours of the morning.

Nancy then decided to give a masked ball and asked us to play for her after we finished our regular job. We arrived at her apartment on the appointed night but so late that some of the guests were already leaving. I can't remember all of those who were there but quite a few of the social celebrities of Venice were among the guests.

Oliver Messel, who had done much stage decoration work for Charles B. Cochran in London, I remember very well because he had his eyelashes done up in silver.

Another man, who, for some reason, was called the Spanish Prince I also remember. During the evening he had lost a little box whose contents seemed vital to his enjoying the night. For another reason I also remember him. He and his friend, a man who looked rather like a priest, tried to inveigle me into a washroom that already seemed pretty well occupied. At that time I did not know what they wanted. I do now. I escaped the ordeal, however, by attaching myself to Nancy.

The party ended at daybreak in a downpour of rain. Although I felt rather sad for some reason as I stood at the window watching the rain, everyone else seemed in the highest spirits as they left.

I stayed behind. . . . We had breakfast together later in the day. It was my first experience of that kind.

CHAPTER VI

An Undefinable Attraction

ALTHOUGH IT WAS a new experience in my life, I have since learned to regret that breakfast. For me, it was a curious affair and at that time it caused the admiration I had for this extremely interesting woman to deepen.

As the event took place I could hardly make myself believe that such an incident could occur in my life. There I was, having late breakfast with a white woman. Even a month before that I would never have dreamed that I would ever see Venice much less be the guest of a white woman in her own home.

During the course of the meal the conversation turned to the Constitution of the United States. Of all odd subjects to discuss this seemed the most unlikely but much to her amusement I found myself explaining this famous document to her in what I considered to be a very scholarly manner.

But to be regretted later or not, this was probably one of the most enjoyable meals I have ever eaten. The entire incident had been pleasant and as we parted that morning I was doubly sure all my resolutions would be discarded for I knew I was infatuated with a white woman.

I have no way of explaining exactly how I justified such a decision in my own mind. Something stronger than all of the will I could command swept me along at such a speed it was impossible for me to direct my actions in the manner I had always considered the most sane.

Somehow I felt this woman had something that I had never discovered in any other person. I greatly admired her intelligence, experience and certain independence of thought.

Later, I learned of other characteristics but at that moment I thought of her as a wonderful creature and allowed myself to be held by an invisible power she seemed to possess.

Shortly after Nancy's party we played for a barge party given by Elsa Maxwell, one of the most noted America hostesses in Europe. At that time it was one of the most magnificent affairs I had ever seen and everyone of any social importance in Venice was invited.

As the summer continued some interesting incidents took place in the nightclub where we were playing. One of these was a fight between a lone German, the whole staff of waiters and the other three members of the band.

The German gave good account of himself but the odds were against him. The interesting aspect for me was watching the efforts of the American Consul to get Nancy out of the area of action despite her insistence on staying and seeing the last blow struck.

Another was a very strange encounter between myself, the son of an Italian nobleman then living in Venice, and a waiter. All three of us were potential lovers of Nancy's. Strange as it may seem we three met in the kitchen off the ballroom for drinks. Nancy made the fourth of the party and it turned to be a crowd. I did not realize the position of the other two men at the time.

Nancy, of course, understood everything and handled the situation like a general. There was quite a lot of side-play by each of us. The poor waiter was at a disadvantage because he did not dare come out openly against the son of a powerful Italian nobleman.

As for myself, the number of drinks I had taken left me with the feeling of caring for "nobody or nothing." Probably because of that, the young aristocrat won. I remember how angry I was as I watched the Italian assist Nancy into her gondola at the end of the street.

In a light drizzle of rain I wandered home, impatiently raging at my defeat. I cursed everything in sight: my luck, the two Italians and even myself for becoming involved in such an affair.

Usually such self-administered reprimands are forgotten the following day when the hang-over disappears but the incident did cause me to seriously consider my position. There I was, a black man mixed up in a three cornered affair with two white men. And all over a white woman. To make it worse one of the men was the son of a count in a foreign country.

I reasoned that I was a fool; that I had placed myself in a precarious position. I decided that the affair was too danger-ous for me; I vowed then and there to retrace my steps toward the path of good judgement from which I had strayed.

The poor waiter seemed to be in a bad enough position but he was an Italian and a white man while I was only a musician and had all of the disadvantages of being an alien Negro opposing the son of a rich Italian citizen. I told myself that I was going to get out of the mess.

But I never did. There was that same undefinable attrac-tion, that same pulling force, that same something so intrigu-ing and interesting that I could not shake myself loose.

After that brawl I did know though that any love I might have had for Nancy had been killed. I saw myself as a pawn upon her chessboard of life. I realized I was no longer the king I had imagined myself to be but still I was in the game and I thought in a strategic position. And even though I was only a player in her game I felt I had been cast for an important part.

The proposals she had made led me to believe that my progress would be greater if I saw the end of what had begun. Maybe it was a spirit of adventure, but something would not let me stop there—I wanted to see where it would all lead. But I was determined from that night on to do so in a detached and coolly calculating way. Even if I was going to be used to satisfy some other person's pleasure I felt I was going to enjoy it also. I might lose in the end but the path she followed promised innumerable new things to a black man who had only seen life from a colored man's viewpoint.

The contract for the services of the orchestra ended during the first weeks of October. The other members of the band prepared to return to Paris but I informed them that I was staying behind a few days longer in Venice.

The boys very strongly and wisely advised me against this step, telling me it was very dangerous for me in view of the suspected enmity of the count's son. Victor, another of Nancy's cousins, also advised against my remaining behind and became rather terrified at the thought of us travelling to Paris together. However, in my desire not to break the first link of what promised to be a long chain of interesting events coupled with Nancy's very urgent requests that I stay, I remained behind.

This extended stay only lasted about ten days and it was not a very pleasant one. The warning of my companions constantly rang in my ears. I changed my hotel hoping the move would do me good and allay supposed suspicions but the new proprietor was worse than the old.

Nancy and I became conscious of being watched and I was glad when the day arrived for us to leave for Paris. We had been warned that it would be rather dangerous for us to leave Italy together but we braved the supposed dangers and left for Paris on the same train.

A Fascist military officer occupied the compartment with us. He eyed us very suspiciously and before we had reached Milan his attention to us felt very uncomfortable. He finally asked the conductor what kind of tickets we carried. He was informed that we were international travelers. His interest subsided somewhat after that but he plainly showed his disapproval of a white woman travelling with a black man.

In desperation, in order to be rid of him, we left the train at Milan and stopped there for the night. The next day we continued our journey to Paris without further incident. A great feeling of relief came over me upon passing the frontier into France.

As we neared Paris Nancy began telling me of the difficulties she had been having with a former lover, Louis Aragon, the French writer. I had heard something of the affair in

Venice. They had been close friends for years but it seemed
that on this trip to Venice where he had gone with Nancy
their relations had been very unpleasant. What had caused the
trouble I never learned as it all happened before I met her.
According to Nancy his actions became so obnoxious he was
told to go away and calm down. When that happened he
returned to Paris.

As Nancy approached Paris with me she began to worry
about what might happen when we arrived. She feared Aragon might even be at the station to meet us and make an
unpleasant scene. When the train arrived no Aragon was in
sight but Nancy was in such an excited state that we rushed
off to a small hotel in Montmartre.

All of her premonitions did not worry me in the least.
I felt that I had a perfect right to be where I was and certainly
did not intend to become excited about the situation. Besides,
it was all new to me and I was enjoying the experience.

At the hotel she cautioned me against us going to the
places Aragon was known to frequent. I did not know
whether these fears of hers were justified or not but I never
saw Aragon until weeks later. When I did meet him I found
him to be a very charming and intelligent Frenchman.

In Paris I soon contacted the other members of the orchestra and learned they had been trying to locate me. They
had been worrying about what might have happened in Venice. As soon as I told them nothing out of the ordinary had
taken place they seemed much relieved and asked where I was
staying.

When I refused to tell them they very quickly supposed
that I was living at some prominent hotel and would not give
them my address because I did not want any colored callers.
I was amused at their suppositions but said nothing to make
them alter their opinions.

As a result, the story quickly spread over the black section of Montmartre that I had met a very rich white woman
in Venice and had come to Paris with her. From the stories

that were soon being told in the bars I learned that many persons knew more about the affair than I knew myself.

I said little to refute this gossip for I soon learned that the more I said the more the stories were stretched. On the other hand I was enjoying all the notoriety I had gained from the idle talk. As I had saved a bit of money while in Venice I did my best to act the role thrust upon me.

At that time I knew little about Nancy and nothing about her mother and how wealthy Lady Cunard was supposed to be. I was very fond of the woman but was more on my guard than ever for some of the things that I had heard and things that had happened caused me to be more than cautious.

But the same invisible force that had held me in Venice, the same indescribable something made me continue. I was more than curious to see just where the affair would lead. Too, I felt sure of myself and believed that by adopting a cautious attitude I could at least enjoy whatever the future held in store for me. So despite the warnings against such actions that still rumbled deep down within me, I followed the trail I had started.

Nancy had business to conduct in London and informed me that she must shortly leave for England. It was then that the question of an apartment for me came up. She stated that I really should have one and offered to pay half the rent.

This struck me as extraordinary. Since our first meeting I had never asked for help of any kind and had certainly never broached the subject of money gifts. I did not need or really want an apartment but agreed to her proposal, thinking it would not do to argue about a few hundred francs at that stage of our friendship.

With her parting instructions that I find an apartment began my many experiences in regard to Nancy's disposition in money matters. I was to learn that she was (and still is I suppose) the perfect example of a person who is penny wise and dollar foolish.

I have seen her spend many hundreds of francs buying

drinks for nobodies and the next day complain because a meal cost ten francs. The manner in which she handled her money was to me most amazing.

I recall at one time meeting a young professor of languages in Paris by the name of Samuel Beckett who later went to Dublin University to teach. Nancy became very interested in this man and he did have a very charming personality.

Subsequently, as we were journeying to London, Nancy told me she had given the professor quite a large sum of money. Naturally I was surprised because he was a very recent acquaintance. When I inquired why she gave it to him she stated it was because he seemed to be in need; that she felt like doing it.

During the talk that followed I made the assertion that she was all too willing to buy friendships; that by giving the money she therefore placed people under obligation to her.

"You are jealous of my giving away my money," she countered. "You probably imagine there will be less for you."

A thought like that had never entered my head for at no time during our relationship was personal financial gain any part of my thoughts. But more of this angle later.

So I went ahead and rented an apartment. Once in the place, however, I could not help but reconsider my position. In almost every room I found something to remind me that I was now doing practically everything I had vowed I would never do. I tried not to think about it too much and was glad when the band secured a contract with The Plantation, a new nightclub that had opened in Montmartre.

When Nancy returned a few weeks later she informed me that she was really only passing through Paris on the way to Chapelle-Réanville, a village near Paris where she owned a country house. She told me that while in London she had decided to open a private printing press at her house in the country.

While she was perfecting the plans for the press she spent quite a lot of time in Paris. I was busy with my new job but we did see a great deal of each other. It was during these first days at The Plantation that Nancy and I had our first serious quarrel. It was concerning lesbians.

We were walking towards my apartment about 6 A.M. after the club had closed when the subject of our conversation for some unknown reason turned to the question of lady-lovers.

I made some very caustic and uncomplimentary remarks about them and Nancy immediately took exception to everything I had said. A very heated argument followed. She told me flatly that she liked lesbians; had enjoyed their company before and hoped to do so again.

My answer was that I wanted nothing to do with lesbians or anyone who had anything to do with them.

"In that case," Nancy replied, "we had better separate right here."

"Okay," I said, and off she went.

I went on home alone. I was very angry; went straight to bed but not to sleep for shortly afterwards the telephone rang. It was Nancy.

In a very sweet voice she asked me if I did not want her to come and see me.

"Certainly," I answered.

The matter was ended before we ever went to sleep.

Since that time I have met, dined and danced with many lesbians and have had reason to radically change my opinion of them. One's mind can always find dirt if one is really looking for it, I have learned since.

I think I can now number several lesbians among the best friends I have known in Europe. Wonders can be done by forgetting that they are unfortunate enough to have this peculiar quirk and by considering them as human beings like the rest of us. It is not always their fault.

Nancy continued to busy herself with setting up and starting the press in her country place. Called the Hours Press, it started rather inauspiciously but before its final demise a great many privately printed books, pamphlets and poetry were produced there.

At that time I was working under a terrific strain. During the week my time was taken up with my job, the study of French and the piano and on weekends Nancy was always in town. Difficulties and dissensions also arose in the band.

I told Nancy of these and she tried to persuade me to quit work and go to the country with her. I refused at first, declaring to myself I would never allow a woman to "keep" me. After an ugly incident in Montmartre involving a member of our band, however, I changed my decision. The incident, which startled all Paris, was as follows:

Mike, our banjo player, had been on a spree for some days and though he always turned up for work he was usually in a pretty drunken condition.

One night he came to work particularly drunk and expressed his intention of shooting anyone who interfered with him. I cautioned him against doing anything foolhardy but he seemed to grow more and more determined as the night wore on.

At 5 A.M. we finished work and Mike and I left the Plantation together. He invited me into the Costa Bar to have a drink. I refused and left him. The last I saw of him that morning he was staggering noisily into the door of the Costa Bar Cafe.

The same evening I came down the rue Fontaine about seven o'clock and someone asked if I knew that Mike was in jail. I said I did not and then heard for the first time an account of what had happened.

After I left Mike, he went to Brick-Top's place just around the corner from the Costa Bar. There he met Sidney Bechet, another Negro musician. An altercation arose between the two about the musical qualifications of the members of our band and especially about myself.

Bechet made some particularly nasty remarks and Mike struck him in the face. When Bechet attempted to retaliate Mike drew his pistol and threatened to let day-light into

Bechet's body if he attempted to hit back. I have not the slightest doubt that Mike would not have hesitated in shooting Bechet at that moment if he had made the first move to fight.

Bechet, in great anger, left Brick-Top's, went home and got his pistol and came back looking for Mike. By this time Mike had returned to the Costa Bar. When Mike appeared someone told him that Bechet was outside waiting for him with a gun. Mike immediately drew his gun and walked out into the rue Fontaine to meet Bechet.

As soon as Mike appeared in the doorway bullets began to fly. The two men were hardly more than ten feet apart. Both had fully loaded revolvers and they emptied every chamber firing at each other at this close range.

One bullet crashed through the glass door at the Costa Bar, another found a resting place in the foot of Glover Compton, an American Negro musician who is well known to American and English tourists who visit Fred Payne's or Harry's New York Bar. Glover was standing near the door when the shooting started and one of the wild shots crippled him for many months.

An old French woman passing along the street stopped another bullet and still another lodged somewhere in the neck or shoulder of an English girl who was unluckily nearby. The remainder of the shots went wild and neither of the perpetrators of this carnage was scratched.

Mike and Bechet then threw away their now useless weapons and proceeded to finish the battle with their fists. The police were quickly on the spot and carried both of the combatants off to jail. Mike tried to rough it with the police at the station but of course he got the worst of the encounter.

Although the three people hit by the bullets were seriously injured, no fatalities resulted.

Nancy, upon being informed of the affair, immediately interested herself in Mike's behalf. She had, from the Venice days, been very keen on Mike. She frequently remarked about his good looks, etc. I once saw her kiss him one night in

Venice as they sat talking in a window-seat after a dinner party. Her cousins, Edward and Victor, were also great admirers of Mike.

Through her French friend, Aragon, Nancy contacted Henry Torres, the famous French criminal lawyer, and he agreed to defend Mike. Bechet also secured a well qualified attorney to represent him.

When this happened it was winter and cold. Poor Mike was in prison clothed only in his tuxedo. When we finally located him at La Sante prison, Nancy, in cooperation with her cousin Victor, procured him some warmer clothes and supplied him with cigarettes and spending change.

When the trial came up Torres did what he could but the case was hopeless. The judges were very caustic in their remarks concerning the entire affair.

Gene Bullard, former colored boxer, who has trained such famous fighters as Kid Chocolate and Al Brown, was one of the witnesses for the defense but his testimony was somewhat of an enigma. I never understood just what his testimony was about but I am sure it did not help either Mike or Bechet.

They were both sentenced to 15 months imprisonment and fined 10,000 francs each. After serving the 15 months they could not pay their fines so they were both deported.

Some of the colored folks in Montmartre may have thought that Nancy interested herself in Mike's behalf because he was a co-worker of mine. That may be. I thought so at the time.

But in the light of my later experiences I know now that this was not the reason. Nancy and I have often talked of Mike since then and she has always been very exuberant in the expressions of her admiration for his physical appearance.

Often has she said if she had any idea how to locate Mike she would certainly do so, and I believe she would.

CHAPTER VII

Chapelle-Réanville
and the Hours Press

DURING THE FIRST DAYS that Mike spent in jail I finally agreed with Nancy that it might be better for me to go to the country. It was winter and cold, the band had broken up and I was without work.

One thing I did insist on though before finally making the move—that I be allowed to work and receive a regular weekly salary for what I did. Even though my outlook then was none too bright, I would not hear of living there without doing some work. Accordingly, a salary was arranged and the routine of work I was to follow was stipulated.

The chauffeur who brought Nancy's Talbot to call for me the morning I moved seemed very displeased about something. He was a young Frenchman named George who had a record for being a reckless, daredevil driver. He drove to the country like a madman.

I liked Puits Carre, the name of the country place that Nancy had reconstructed, from the very first. It is an old farm house with two out-buildings standing on the easy slope of a hillside. It has a large well, a good garden and some fruit trees.

Well located in the village and about six miles from the railroad, it is admirable for occupancy in the summer but is one of the coldest places I know during the winter. It is modern in every respect except for the heating and that is atrocious.

I learned to love its grounds for the spirit of open friendliness they seemed to possess and the rolling hills of the surrounding countryside. But for the house itself, nothing I can think of connected with Nancy demonstrates more clearly the kind of person she really is.

The plan for its reconstruction was drawn up by Nancy and Aragon. The actual work was also supervised by them. But a great lack of continuity is very evident in the arrangement of the rooms and I found the same curious contradictions there that I have discovered in Nancy's character.

As a matter of fact, it is hard to imagine a more inconveniently arranged house. The kitchen is placed in the middle of the ground floor, two bedrooms are on one side, the diningroom and a large hall on the other.

The kitchen opens only on the front and there is no passage from the hall and the dining room to the bedrooms except through the kitchen, outside and in again or upstairs and down again. We all found this arrangement very trying at times and Nancy was one of the worst grumblers. Scarcely a day passed without her severely criticizing and denouncing something about the place.

She complained of the cold, of the dampness, of the windows, of the heating, of the doors. In fact, she complained of everything and was constantly threatening to sell the place. I think she once put it up for sale but changed her mind about it as she has done about nearly everything else. Now she considers it rather a refuge in these days of financial stress and worries.

My first days at Chapelle-Réanville were very nice and interesting. We took long walks exploring the countryside. I enjoyed these greatly for Nancy was a great walker and companion. There were also short auto rides to nearby cities.

I spent much time reading, for Nancy possessed a splendid library. A piano was secured and I had a lot of time to practice. The two servants, George and his wife, seemed quite enough for the house.

There was also plenty to drink of every description and in spite of the rather curious arrangement of the rooms the house was very comfortable for it was expensively furnished.

So I was in clover. Transported suddenly from all of the excitement of Paris to the absolute calm of the country was a very pleasing change for me.

Too, Nancy was graciousness itself. She was very solicitous of my every need and did everything possible to make me comfortable. I did not regret having left Paris for she succeeded in doing this to a remarkable degree.

I knew if those first weeks we spent together in the country were any criterion of what was to follow I would never regret having set all of my other ideas on the shelf. At that moment the future again looked bright for the way she talked I felt I might yet accomplish big things and complete a life which my race could point to with pride.

As time passed I became more and more fond of the house and its surroundings. At my suggestion Nancy bought paint and I painted the entire exterior of all the buildings and fences with two coats as the new wood on the doors and windows was beginning to show the effects of the damp climate. At all times I tried to convince Nancy of the charm of the place and discouraged her talk of ever selling it.

One night during a regular after-dinner conversation the question of Negroes and conditions affecting them in America came up. I was amazed at Nancy's absolute ignorance about such matters.

But she was interested and eager to learn. I told her of Negro writers; told her where she could get books on and by them. Gradually, she began to build up her library with Negro books. She took a yearly subscription to *The Crisis,* a magazine published by Negroes in New York. American Negro papers also made their appearance.

I was glad and pleased that she showed an interest in my race and thought from the way she talked she really wanted to do something for the Negro cause. I did not have the slightest idea at the time, however, that such a chance topic of conversation would lead to the amazing chain of events which were destined to follow.

One afternoon, shortly after that when I was in Paris,

Nancy asked me to lunch with her on the Champs-Elysees. George, the chauffeur, was to call for us with the car. He arrived an hour late, making some perfunctory excuse.

I was expecting him to be severely taken to task and was mildly surprised at the manner in which Nancy spoke to him about being late. It seemed to me that she was almost apologizing to him.

On another occasion when he was to drive us to the country he arrived one and one-half hours late. Again he was scolded in such a mild manner that my sense of the proper relation between master and servant was somewhat outraged. I spoke to Nancy about it, telling her that she should not allow her chauffeur to choose his own time for keeping an appointment.

The two incidents struck me with a peculiarly unpleasant force. I wondered what this was about for on both occasions George had seemed to care not in the least and always replied in a sulky manner. I said nothing but decided to keep my eyes open.

I had to wait quite a long time before I "saw through" the entire thing. George created a furor one day by driving the car to Paris and not returning or communicating with the house. After a reasonable time for his return had passed telephone inquiries were made. The night passed and still no news from George.

The following day the car was located in a garage George frequented when in Paris. The garage owner was instructed to hold the car and notify the errant George to call the house. When he did call he was promptly fired. His wife left the same day.

Finally, when Anna, an old maid of Nancy's returned to work, I got some light thrown on what looked like a hazy situation and learned why George had refused to take any reprimands seriously. Anna and I became good friends so I talked to her about George, mentioning his strange conduct.

She had seen George after he was discharged and said he remarked that Nancy might be Madame to the rest of her servants but she was just "plain" Nancy to him. I understood the "plain" Nancy expression perfectly and was glad that he was gone.

I said nothing to Nancy but thanked George in my own mind for more or less confirming what I had suspected. Too, he caused me to again do some critical thinking about my own position. By that time I knew I was going to "see it through" but I also knew it was going to be from a more detached viewpoint than ever before.

My feelings toward Nancy did not change a great deal for I had already seen in Venice that she was a woman of many interests and of changing fancies. By assuming a quiet, detached air I felt I could accomplish much more for myself and my race than if I jealously quarrelled about events that had passed.

The press was now going full swing. Nancy had hired a professional craftsman to handle the technical part of the printing. He was a fat little Frenchman by the name of Levy. I am sure he thought well of himself. He slept in the village but had his lunch at the house.

When I first went to the country he was eating lunch with Nancy in the diningroom. But this was changed and Nancy and I had our lunch together thereafter and the printer had his alone in another room. I am sure he never got over the change.

After that there were many unpleasant incidents between ourselves and the printer until the end of his work that spring. However my duties usually kept me out of contact with M. Levy. He spent all of his time in the print shop and when I was not packing and shipping books from the library I was either practicing or reading. I only saw him when I had an occasion to go to the press room and that was not very often. He became very disagreeable toward the end of the season and we breathed a sigh of relief when his time expired.

During the winter there had been several house guests, among whom were included the writer Richard Aldington and his friend, Bridget Patmore. The mention of his name

*Henry, unidentified friend, and Nancy on a musical outing. Photo courtesy
Anne Chisholm.*

recalls to my mind two incidents which took place; one during the Christmas holidays the preceding winter and the other
in the spring.

It was while I was still working at the Plantation in Paris
and living in the apartment that the first occurred. Aldington
came to my place one day in search of Nancy as they were
great friends at the time.

He was in a suicidal mood; very wild eyes and swearing
to do himself in. It seemed as though his affair of the heart
with Bridget had gone wrong and life was not worth living
any longer.

We succeeded in pacifying him, however, and showed
him the road back to reason. The last I heard from Aldington
he was living happily and enjoying the fruits of his successful
labors.

The other took place one afternoon on a cafe terrace in
Montparnasse. Richard Aldingon, Nancy, Bridget Patmore
and some newspaperman whose name escapes me at the moment, and I were together when drinks were ordered.

Nancy selected gin. When the drinks arrived Nancy remarked about the peculiar odor of the gin that had been served to her. Each of us in turn had a smell of the glass. None of the others could recognize the liquid. When I had a whiff of the glass I immediately pronounced its contents American moonshine. Just plain raw corn liquor that is known as White Mule because of the kick it carries with it.

The newspaperman immediately grabbed the incident and made a story of it. It was printed in newspapers all over America not only because persons prominent in the literary world were sitting at the table but also because of the remarkable enterprise of American bootleggers who had been selling their liquor in France as gin.

Louis Aragon, Nancy's ex-lover, was also down at the house in the country. He seemed to be a well bred French boy; was very handsome, spoke excellent English and in all struck me as being very intelligent.

He had been Nancy's lover for a long time but it was all finished now for she always said she never returned to a lover once she had left him. In her case the new love always definitely replaced the old. There was no rekindling of old fires with her. My case alone, I suppose, was the exception.

Aragon had found himself another sweetheart and this brought about an amusing situation. This new love of Aragon's knew Nancy and she was determined that Aragon should never see Nancy again.

On her side Nancy could not see why she should not see her former lover and now friend again. Some amusing skirmishes followed but Aragon's new love won the fray so Aragon passed entirely from the stage, much to the disgust of Nancy.

The latter part of the winter and the spring I had spent at Chapelle-Réanville had taught me a great deal. For one thing I had learned what it meant to be on intimate terms with prominent white people and considered as an equal in every way.

In that respect I think I forgot my color the same as they seemingly did. As I recall it, I was conscious of nothing other

than being the same kind of man as the others whose company
I enjoyed. At night when I was alone in my bed I often
wondered why they accepted me on equal terms and yet in
my own country I was considered different from others. I
could not help but long for the freedom of my people in my
country that I was enjoying in Europe.

I also learned a great deal more about Nancy. I learned
of her moods, her insatiable desire to always be doing something, of the quick-fire decisions she could make, of her will
to finish what she had started regardless of the circumstances.

When the summer of 1929 arrived the press was closed
and my first trip to London with Nancy was scheduled. A
few weeks previously I had been in an accident. While driving
the car I crashed into another automobile which was occupied
by three Frenchmen.

We later received a note to the effect that the driver of
the other car wanted to be paid for the damages done. Knowing that everything was fully covered by insurance we ignored this and left for London.

I travelled across the Channel with mixed feelings and
no little trepidation. I knew a great deal about England and
the color question from my many Negro musician acquaintances. I was rather doubtful about just what was going to
happen.

On the train from Folkestone to London an Englishman
left the table in the dining-car as we took our seats. However,
that had no significance and I was glad to see him go.

In London there was no space available for me at The
Tower, which was Nancy's pet hotel. The proprietor, a Mr.
Stulik, said that on account of the big race (the derby), every
room was occupied. I think this was true because I stayed at
the hotel on later occasions.

Failing to find a room there for myself—Nancy's room
already being reserved—we took a taxi to find a hotel where
I could stay. We certainly had our troubles and our experiences
confirmed all I had heard about the color bar in London.

We were refused at place after place. Finally, when tempers were rising and Nancy for the first time was facing the fact that color prejudice did exist in England, we followed the suggestion of the taxi driver and went to a hotel in Bloomsbury. I was taken in there without question.

In special cases like this, London and England are infinitely worse for colored people than New York or other cities in the United States. It is the shock of the terrible humiliation from being refused so unexpectedly that cuts. And all because of one's color.

The average American colored person does not expect racial prejudice in England or Europe and when he or she is suddenly confronted with it surprise is hardly the word to express their feelings.

Our first few days in London were devoted to the usual sightseeing and getting the "feel" of the city, at least for me. Nancy was as busy as a bee. Her mother, Lady Cunard, had to be seen by Nancy practically every day at some time; either for lunch, tea or dinner. Then there were scores of friends to be contacted, and lastly, myself. The necessity of seeing her mother seemed to offer the greatest inconvenience to Nancy—a new side of Nancy I was learning.

She disliked doing this seemingly most natural thing very much and did it like a person taking a nasty dose of medicine.

We got about London a great deal and no unpleasant incidents occurred. I met no colored people at all but I saw a lot of Nancy's friends and was invited somewhere every night.

Among others I met a Mr. and Mrs. Otto Theis, very charming literate people. Also there was Wyn Henderson, a woman connected with the publishing business, who was to play a big role in later events. We spent some six or eight weeks in London on this trip and I enjoyed myself thoroughly.

Upon our return to France, I discovered I had received a summons from the court at Evreux as a result of the automobile accident; that the court had met and because of my non-appearance I had been sentenced to one month in prison and fined 10,000 francs. All of this was through the failure of a servant to forward the notice for my appearance to England. The court was informed of this and it was decided to call the case again in the fall.

Nancy and I then spent a short time in Paris where I met H. R. H. Prince Tovalou, a black pretender to the throne of some African kingdom. Nancy knew the pretender through the Princess Violet Murat, the wife of a man belonging to a French family famed for its love and war exploits.

This Negro pretended to be a lawyer and Nancy immediately went into my accident case with him. After much preliminary talk he agreed to conduct my defense in the autumn. I had strong suspicious of this Negro but left the matter entirely to Nancy. After that was settled we left for Bordeaux.

I remember having a very serious argument over the dinner table in Bordeaux so we left the next day for Le Bugue where we spent the remainder of what proved to be a very hectic summer. We travelled around much of the countryside visiting caves, chateaux, etc. Nancy was writing most of the time and I was studying French. Leaving there early in the fall we travelled south, visiting Biarritz, Saint-Jean-de-Luz and Spain.

In Saint-Jean-de-Luz I met Yvonne, a great friend of Nancy's. She was once a great beauty and had made a name for herself on the French stage. When I met her she was a hopeless drug addict, suffering terribly because of her inability to obtain drugs. She was trying to get relief from inadequate substitutes.

In desperation it was decided that we all go visit her doctor who was a great distance away. The three of us with a huge dog took a taxi to journey some 300 kilometers. As it happened the trip was practically useless as the doctor refused to provide drugs, at least the kind and the quantity desired. In addition, I lost a new walking stick which I highly prized because Nancy had given it to me.

The poor girl died later enroute to Italy after presumably being cured in a nursing home in Switzerland. I still have a lovely pair of bedroom slippers and a pair of red Basque trousers which this beautiful but unfortunate woman gave me.

We stayed in Saint-Jean-de-Luz until practically everyone had left and then journeyed southward, stopping just short of Spain in a great, dismal empty hotel. The season for guests at all of these places was long past and the chill of winter was in the air.

After a short sojourn in the north of Spain this southern journey ended. We headed back for Paris and went immediately to the country as my court case regarding the automobile accident was scheduled to be heard at Evreux, a town near our village.

The Negro, Prince Tovalou, whom Nancy had retained to conduct my defense, had been contacted during the summer and arrangements were made for him to arrive at Chapelle-Réanville the day before the trial started.

Nancy and I were naturally anxiously awaiting his arrival. I had held strong suspicious of this man all along so I bet Nancy he would not put in an appearance. Sure enough, he did not so we were forced to go to court without an attorney to defend me.

At the court room we met the lawyer for the insurance company and he agreed to do what was possible. After some extremely embarrassing moments the one month's prison sentence that had previously been passed against me was cancelled. I was also fined 100 francs and ordered to pay 10,000 francs to the other parties. The insurance company promptly assumed all liability.

This of course ended all of our relations with Tovalou whom we later learned was a person of very dubious standing and had no right whatsoever to represent anyone before any court of law.

Princess Murat, who had introduced Nancy to Tovalou, had some uncomplimentary things to say of him and I personally wrote him a letter, telling him he was a disgrace to the black race.

The first time I ever saw Tovalou he was with Nancy at

the Plantation nightclub in Montmarte. The last time I saw him was at the Hampton School Choir Concert in Paris. He endeavored to explain his non-appearance at the court at that time but I turned a deaf ear. I have since heard that he has been in prison for some offense or other.

By that time I had learned still more about Nancy. To my disappointment I had discovered that she was a very selfish person. Her likes and desires came before everything. Her whole life was (and still is I suppose) controlled and actuated by one idea—her own selfish pleasure and gratification. As soon as anything ceased to give her personal pleasure she was finished with it.

I also discovered how tight and close she was with money. My first experiences with this trait began in Paris and showed itself in the house at Chapelle-Réanville. Then, when we started travelling about together, I had to get my cigar and drink money from her as the need for each item arose.

The only times that I ever received any real money from Nancy were when I was going to America and when she bought me a car but even in these transactions the undercurrent of selfishness could always be felt. I had also learned of the slumbering enmity she felt for her mother which was later to awake, and burst into such a vicious flame.

At this point of our relations I was also beginning to wonder if Nancy was as wonderful as *all that*. I am not a very passionate animal in any case and she never appealed to me greatly from a sexual standpoint.

In addition, never in my life have I been thoroughly in love with a white woman. Their desires, their likes, their psychology of life are entirely different from that of a colored person. There are certain points upon which all peoples can meet and enjoy each other's company but the true characteristics of the colored and the whites are as different as those of a true Parisian and a New Yorker.

True, I have associated with white women in Europe to a certain extent and have certainly spent many pleasant moments with them. But my pleasure is to be with a colored

woman. A colored woman has always been my sole companion since returning to Europe this last time with the exception
of the last few weeks with Nancy which were the final cause
of this book.

CHAPTER VIII

Troubling Affairs . . .

A ND THE AFFAIR still continued. Back in Paris I once again "took inventory" as it were and though there was not much to record as "in hand" I decided to stick. The business of more or less just hanging on was beginning to become irksome however.

Still, I had not heard from my wife for months and months; all of the connections I had in America had been severed and many of the friends I had known in Paris had either returned to the United States or were working in other parts of Europe.

So I stuck. I was determined to see the end of it; to see if all of the bright promises that had been made to me would ever be fulfilled. In the eyes of many I was still on the top of the heap but by that time I was beginning to have my doubts about the size of the heap.

Once more in Paris the question of the press still remained. The program for the winter of 1929 and the spring of 1930 was extremely heavy. Personally, I thought Nancy was trying to do too much and could see she was tiring of the whole business. I could feel that she wanted more freedom than the press would allow and sure enough she began casting about for a way out.

To do this she conceived of the dubiously brilliant idea of moving the entire press to Paris. I mildly tried to discourage her from doing so but my words were wasted. That indomitable spirit of hers, whether right or wrong, exerted itself.

To further irritate matters a serious break came about between us at this time. She had been showing little signs of being rather tired of me and we had exchanged some rather acrid words about my not doing anything. She accused me of being lazy, saying that I ought to get to work playing somewhere.

Somehow, I had realized for many months that such an outburst was coming but I had decided to wait and see exactly what it would bring with it. After all, she was the one who had persuaded me to stop trying to find work in the first place and I wanted to see just how long she would hold to one decision.

One afternoon shortly after this we were having lunch in Montparnasse with two of her boy friends, Walter and John—two fairies. For some reason she was feeling nasty towards me and I was in no saintly mood myself.

She cracked at me again and again about going to work.

"Why don't you get something to do?" was the essence of some of her remarks, and "You know you should go to work."

"By heaven, I will," I replied and left. Although I had willingly let myself in for what I felt was coming she was going a little too far. I went straight to the owner of the Bateau Ivre and went to work immediately playing and singing every night at a good salary.

The press in the meantime arrived in Paris and was installed in the rue Guenegaud. After many complications there still remained the question of finding printers. Everything eventually moved along but how or why is more than I can understand to this day. I was busy with my job and little at the press.

Usually when I finished work at the Bateau Ivre I went straight home and to bed. The club often remained open after the music had stopped at about 2 A.M. but at that late hour I was too tired to become particularly interested in anything other than sleep.

One of these nights when I went to bed early I was awakened about four o'clock by loud knocking at my door. Upon opening it who should unceremoniously march in but

Nancy and Eugene MacCown, an American painter living in Paris.

Both were literally blind drunk. They talked incoherently and began stumbling all around my room. I very naturally wanted to know where on earth they had been and how they had managed to get into such an awful state.

In a very drunken manner they told me the following story:

They had been "doing" Paris that night and had finally wound up at the place where I worked. They ordered a last drink. This last one "for the road" had knocked them out completely. They both swore that the manager of the place had put dope in their glasses. Until the last they insisted this was true and hence their helpless conditions.

I never believed a word of it. To me it looked like a plain everyday drunk.

There was a private bath attached to my room and after some drunken vagaries Nancy proceeded to take a hot bath. In the meantime Eugene wanted to know if it was possible for him to stay the night in my room as he was very drunk and lived a long distance away. Seeing his condition, I consented.

He got into bed with me. Nancy was busily engaged taking her bath. Whether because of his drunken state or not I shall never know but no sooner had Eugene gotten into bed with me than an abnormal sex desire on his part started to make itself known.

He made solicitous overtures which I hotly resented. He began to pull at my pajamas. I became very angry indeed, threatening him with bodily injury if he did not stop.

He did, drunkenly mumbling that I did not seem to care for him. Had he not been very drunk I would have thrown him out.

Nancy then emerged from the bathroom and to my perfect astonishment got into bed also, placing me in the middle.

"Damn," I thought, "her room is next door. Why in the

name of Heaven does she have to get in here? This will never do."

They were both so drunk, however, that they went straight to sleep. I slipped out from between them, dressed and went off to Montmarte to spend the rest of the night, thinking how unlike themselves people can be when they are drunk.

I returned to the hotel about eleven o'clock the next morning. They were somewhat more sober and sensible by that hour so Eugene dressed and left for his home.

The incident did not seem to be anything extraordinary for Nancy. She made no comment on the matter except to insist that the manager of the Bateau Ivre had drugged her and Eugene.

She hated the manager from that night and absolutely refused to enter the place again.

The manager of the Bateau Ivre, who was supposed to be a Russian baron, sensed her hostility. In an endeavor to be friendly he sent her a gorgeous bouquet.

Upon its arrival Nancy immediately threw the flowers out the window and consigned the supposed baron to the domain ruled by Satan.

At that time Nancy was spending a great deal of her time in Montmartre. She was away from the hotel a great deal and when I would see her she would act very strange. I knew something was afoot but I could not figure what it was. Nancy had acted strangely on many occasions and usually I overlooked such incidents, ascribing it to her changeable moods.

But this time I knew something different had taken place for her actions were so utterly unlike what I had experienced before. I decided to set my traps to capture the secret. But I can honestly say what I did was in no way motivated by jealousy.

I had known Nancy too long and thought I understood her too well to become jealous of any other man. The attitude I had adopted ruled out such things. I was very interested because her actions were so entirely different from what I had noticed before.

I began running down the secret by going to Montmartre more often. It was not long before one of the traps snapped. Among other things I learned that a colored orchestra was playing at the Grand Ecart, a nightclub. The pianist, whom I later learned was Dan Parish, was a big blue-black Negro and a very fine musician.

The solution of the whole thing was that Nancy had fallen passionately in love with this Negro and evidently he had fallen just as much in love with her.

The colored boys in Montmartre naturally saw the two together and knowing about me, they began whispering and buzzing. My traps caught all of the whispers and buzzes. I found out almost everything.

Then too, Nancy's maid, Anna, who was very fond of me, told me some other facts that gave me the exact truth of the situation. I never mentioned it to Nancy but I knew her affair with Dan was a real scorcher.

It was hot. She was out of her mind about the boy and it continued for about three or more months.

In the meantime I was quietly working away, saving money and seeing Nancy for dinner only now and then.

Yet I must admit frankly that I was greatly hurt and humiliated by this affair with Dan. It was the first colored man she had become attached to that I knew about. There have been many since.

I was not in love with Nancy and I was not jealous but I had a great deal of pride and to have people laughing at me and considering me a fool was not pleasant.

Nancy handled a great deal of money at that time. She was considered very rich and everyone knew of the wealth of her mother, Lady Cunard. Thus, I was supposed to be in velvet. For a long time I had sort of revelled in this adoration from the colored folks until I had begun to imagine that I was something pretty good. It was a terrific shock to me to realize that she had fallen in love with another Negro. I was terribly depressed over all of this and drank a great deal in an attempt to soothe my feelings.

About the time her mad passion had reached white heat I informed Nancy that I had decided to return to America for a visit. I had not been back for longer than I cared to recall and as I had saved a little money I thought this the best time to make the trip. I argued it would give me a chance to "clear my mind" and at the same time take me out of an embarrassing situation.

Countee Cullen, one of the best known Negro poets, and some of his white friends were in my apartment on the same day and offered to assist in making my arrangements.

Nancy got me on the phone from God knows where and begged me to go to Chapelle-Réanville and wait for her before leaving. I had to go down to the house anyway to gather some of my belongings so I agreed. I did not mind having Anna's company for a few days anyway.

In two or three days after I had gone to the country Nancy arrived. A long, involved discussion followed when I told her I had definitely made up my mind to return home for a visit. In the end, the same pulling force, the same indescribable attraction I had first discovered in Venice triumphed. I dropped my plan to go to America and we returned to Paris together. I went back to work.

The love affair with Dan then began to cool off. I learned later that there had been some terrific rows between them, some about me, and that Dan had threatened to kill himself. At any rate Dan went to Cannes to work.

Shortly afterwards Nancy had some business to attend to on the Riviera and she went to visit Dan in Cannes. She was gone three or four days. When she returned no one had to tell me that the affair was over.

During all of this time I never mentioned that I knew anything out of the ordinary was happening and she seemed to take it for granted that I would not say anything.

Soon after this I asked Nancy to buy me a car. I had seen a beautiful model on display just down the boulevard from where we were staying. I think I must have chosen just the right moment to make the request.

She seemed pretty well used up after the affair with Dan and, not being quite sure what I was going to do, she consented. In a few days I was driving my lovely car around Paris enjoying the admiring looks and comments it aroused.

I learned later, however, that Nancy was also buying the car for her own use as I practically became her chauffeur and the car was used for every conceivable purpose, both for pleasure and the press.

Nancy's first car was a Talbot; but it gave so much trouble that she sold it. That car was a gift from her mother. With the money she had realized on the sale of the Talbot she bought the car for me.

As in the case with Dan, Nancy seemed to take almost everything where her actions were concerned for granted. In a very curious way she more or less imagined herself above reproach and whenever possible did as she wished regardless of how her actions affected other persons close to her.

Thus, on very short notice it was decided that we make another trip to London in December 1930. We were all packed and prepared to leave the hotel when Nancy received a telegram from Sir Thomas Beecham, the English conductor and composer.

Sir Thomas advised her that it had become known in London by Lady Cunard that Nancy was interested in the career of a Negro musician and that she was bringing him over to London to further his musical education.

Sir Thomas, who is one of the greatest conductors in the world and a member of the famous Beecham pill family, is a great friend of Lady Cunard and of course knew Nancy very well. He therefore naturally concluded that he had the right to advise her against the idea of bringing a colored man to London at that particular time. The telegram coming as it did out of a clear sky and at the moment we were leaving caused no little consternation.

After a brief discussion of the matter, however, we decided to continue the trip as per schedule. I was not perturbed in the slightest.

This visit to London was a business trip. We stayed at the Tower Hotel as we usually did when we went to London.

On the second or third day of our stay there I came into the hotel and asked for a key to the front door as I did not want to be ringing for entrance every time I came in.

Mr. Stulik, the manager, was sent for. He appeared flushed and excited, asking in a hushed voice: "Where is Nancy?" I replied that I did not know and asked about the door key.

"No," he said, "not now. I must see Nancy. You go quickly to your room and wait there."

He seemed very nervous and upset about something. I went to my room wondering what the devil was the matter. Very soon afterwards Nancy arrived and I could hear a very lively exchange of words between her and Stulik downstairs.

Presently she came up looking very angry.

"Pack your things," she said, "we are leaving this hotel immediately."

I was dumbfounded.

"What is the matter?" I asked.

This is what had happened:

Lady Cunard, according to Stulik, had learned that I was at the Tower with Nancy and had informed him either in person or through some other means that if he permitted me to remain in his hotel with Nancy she would see to it that he *got the works.*

Therefore, Stulik, who was a foreigner and had been unfortunate enough to be interned during the war, became terrified at this threat coming from such an important personage as Her Ladyship. He told Nancy I would have to go.

Nancy was furious at this and immediately told him that if I went she would go also. She was one of Stulik's oldest and best customers. He naturally did not wish to lose her patronage but his fear of what Her Ladyship might do was overpowering. We left the hotel without leaving an address.

We later heard from the waiters at the hotel that detectives had made inquiries about our whereabouts and that I was in danger of being deported.

Nancy was very angered over all of this, and she expressed the hatred she held for her mother to me in no uncertain terms.

I was absolutely unruffled. I was not disturbed by any thoughts of being deported. I think this incident was the final wedge that caused the definite break between Nancy and her mother.

Trouble had been brewing, at least from Nancy's side, between the two for many moons and this was the climax.

On another occasion in London we were invited to lunch by Tony Gouneveris, a wealthy South American, who was also a friend of Lady Cunard's. The preceding day, Nancy had casually mentioned to Her Ladyship that she was lunching with Tony.

There were four of us at the lunch. Nancy, Tony, a son of Oscar Wilde, and myself. Nancy and Tony were laughingly discussing Her Ladyship when someone asked me jokingly if I would like to meet Lady Cunard. I replied with a very positive no.

At that very moment an automobile drew up at the door and Tony, looking through the window, recognized it as belonging to Her Ladyship.

"My God, Nancy" he cried, "here is your mother! What shall we do?"

Utter confusion reigned for a moment. I quickly saved the situation by telling Tony that I would not permit Her Ladyship to see me and immediately went upstairs.

Lady Cunard came in, remained for a few moments, and left, taking Nancy with her. I descended from my refuge and the meal was resumed.

Some thirty minutes later we were surprised by the return of Nancy. She had her mother drive her to Hamstead, presumably to see some friend and concocting some likely story, had succeeded in getting rid of her mother. She had returned as quickly as possible. This incident did not improve Nancy's feelings toward Her Ladyship but the lunch terminated in a very light-hearted and good-humored manner. Nancy was very angry that her mother had tried to spy on her so we only remained in London for a few days after the incident, returning to Paris.

Hardly had we crossed the Channel when Nancy received a letter from her mother stating that Her Ladyship intended to spend a few days at Le Touquet, the fashionable resort on the coast and much visited by English people. Naturally, Lady Cunard wanted her daughter to visit her.

It was with exceeding reluctance that Nancy decided to go and it turned out to be my job to drive her up there in my new car. When we arrived I stopped at a hotel in Paris Plage, which is almost a part of Le Touquet. Nancy went to stay with her mother in a large fashionable hotel near the casino in Le Touquet proper.

It is hard to imagine what Lady Cunard's reactions would have been had she known that I saw Nancy every day for an hour or so. We motored around Le Touquet and the surrounding countryside. Fortunately, never once did we see Her Ladyship although we came perilously near doing so on one occasion.

On the morning we left Paris Plage, Nancy arrived at my hotel about eight o'clock in a very intoxicated condition. She told me she had spent the entire night in the casino. I believed her for she slept in the car practically the entire return trip to Paris.

CHAPTER IX

. . . And Improbable Doings

BACK IN PARIS, Nancy again began to frequent her old haunts. As in most cases, I made no comment for such actions nearly always ended in arguments of a nature that were anything but pleasant. She went her way and I went mine but underneath it all there seemed to be something which held us together.

It is impossible for me to state in so many words just what she possessed that attracted me to such an extent and I imagine it would be just as hard for her to give specific reasons why she continued to associate with me. I have no excuses to offer for the life I was then leading for it was of my own choice and I feel fairly certain Nancy would say the same thing about herself if asked.

But in any case, during her wanderings around Montmartre, she met Bob Scanlon, a former Negro prize fighter. During his active career in the ring Scanlon was supposed to have been a good fighter and had seen service in the French army during the world war.

He is a very black Negro and that pleased Nancy very much for the darker a colored man was the more she liked him. She often told me she wished that I was darker.

But outside of his color I could never understand why Nancy liked Bob. He was illiterate and hardly what one would call cultured. I have read some of the letters he wrote Nancy and besides being filled with grammatical mistakes they were practically illegible.

I don't know what his real feelings towards her were but his letters expressed undying love and a wish to have her with him always. Personally, I felt very sorry for poor Bob. I cast no reflections upon his sincerity whatsoever but I did think him foolish to even say he had fallen in love with a white woman when he knew there was not a ghost of a chance that anything would ever come of it. And because of the real feelings I knew Nancy possessed about the man I considered her actions more or less contemptible.

I learned of the affair purely by accident. One afternoon Walter Lowenfels, an American poet then living in Paris, and I went to the press where we thought Nancy could be found.

We knocked on the door. Nancy, in a very impatient voice, demanded to know who was there. We made known our identity. She angrily opened the door and told us to go away as she was busy.

I was definitely startled by what I saw when she opened the door. First of all, I saw Bob Scanlon seated in a chair, just out of my direct vision. Secondly, Nancy was clad only in a sort of chemise or underskirt that was tucked around her legs sort of bloomer fashion.

She was flushed and breathing rather hard.

I could not imagine what was going on and was very surprised to see Bob there.

Upon inquiry she later told me that she was taking boxing lessons from this ex–prize fighter. Of all the things on earth I could imagine her doing this was the most improbable. But it was actually true.

However, Nancy had to get beyond the bounds of the purely professional so apparently an affair developed.

At about that time a privately produced film called "L'Age d'Or" was showing in Paris. It was an extremely sexy film and very anti-religious. One of the final scenes showed Christ leaving what was presumably a brothel, followed by an apparently raped and outraged woman.

The next scene showed Christ re-entering the brothel to kill the woman and then coming out again, apparently well satisfied with what he had done.

Nancy took me to see this show. The film caused considerable excitement in Paris. There were one or two riots in the theatre, causing considerable damage to the screen and the furnishings. These were followed by a loud protest against the film in a certain section of the press. Finally it was confiscated by the Government.

There seemed to have been three copies of the film, however. One of these escaped the hands of the law and was held somewhere in secret.

Nancy found this out and became obsessed with the desire to show this remaining copy privately in England. She combed all Paris in an effort to locate this film. Naturally she encountered every sort of obstacle. Difficulties of every sort arose. She raved and ranted at her inability to procure it. She stated that it was one of the ambitions of her life to procure and show this film in England. With her characteristic pugnacity she refused to give up.

Eventually, she succeeded in locating the film through the influence of friends and acquaintances and secured it. I am sure the amount of money involved was a considerable sum.

The film came out of hiding and it was decided that the safest method of transporting it to London was by air. The necessary arrangements were concluded and we hurried over to London to await its arrival.

During this period the affair with Bob Scanlon evidently proceeded apace. Although Nancy never mentioned it I was sure the "boxing lessons" were still being given by the ex–prize fighter.

Nancy spent some anxious days in London waiting for the film which came along in due time. The job of securing a theatre for the showing came next. After much scurrying around one was found and arrangements were made for a preliminary showing in order to test the sound apparatus.

On the evening prior to this showing Nancy informed me that she was going to spend the night with Bimbo, a young lesbian she had met before. I knew that some sort of intimacy had grown up between them but I said nothing.

Although I had changed my ideas about many other

things, I still clung to my previous decision that the least said
to Nancy about her own actions the better. As for my own
personal feelings, I don't think there was anything Nancy
could do or say at that time which would greatly surprise me.
I might have been surprised at myself for some of the things
I was doing but my foot was in the affair so deeply I feared
it would cause more pain to extract the foot than the ending
of it all was worth.

So I took Nancy's announcement as a matter of course.
As a result, she asked me to call for her the following morning
in time for us to reach the theatre for the test showing at
eleven o'clock.

I accordingly presented myself at Bimbo's flat about ten
in the morning. Bimbo was furious at what she considered
my unwarranted and jealous interruption of her rendezvous
with Nancy. Although I would have enjoyed saying a great
deal, I refused to argue with her so the incident passed.

Invitations were then sent to a select few to come and
see the picture free of charge. The night of the show arrived.
Nancy asked me to distribute a bill to the audience which
gave something of the history of the film. This I agreed to do.

One of the first persons to arrive was Bimbo. While the
theatre was filling with a very curious audience, Nancy was
flitting here and there, greeting her guests.

I was rather pompously seeing that everyone had a program and happened to be near the entrance when a big black
man appeared in the doorway. It was none other than Bob
Scanlon.

He seemed quite taken aback on seeing me and he
showed it. Hesitatingly, he entered. Nancy quite suavely indicated that Bob and I sit together during the show while she
turned her attentions entirely to Bimbo. I had very little to
say and Bob had less.

The show finished. Many of the comments were quite
uncomplimentary and I don't think many of those who attended were at all pleased.

From a personal viewpoint, aside from some fairly good

photography in spots the picture was very poorly done. What Nancy's reactions were to the criticisms, I never knew.

After the show, Bob Scanlon quickly went away. I could see disappointment all over Nancy's face when he left. I was slightly amused at that but did my laughing all to myself.

Nevertheless, she invited a party of us, including Bimbo and myself, to accompany her to an exclusive nightclub to which she belonged. After getting settled at the club I noticed that Nancy seemed very agitated. She ordered drinks for the party and in a few moments asked to be excused. Giving Bimbo (mind you, not me) enough money to pay for the bill, Nancy left.

When time came to settle the waiter stated he could not accept money from anyone who was not a member of the club. As none of the party were members, a delicate situation presented itself. But we left the club, Bimbo leaving money to cover the bill on the table.

I did not see Nancy again for some 48 hours or so and I did not care a great deal after the events that had just passed. Where she went or what she did I never asked but I had a very good idea.

Nancy was like that. Her mind was continually working on some scheme and she never seemed extremely happy unless she was doing something or going somewhere.

An example of some of the "unusual" things she thought of doing was making a trip to Africa with me. When she asked me about it I always replied in the affirmative, not for once thinking such a thing would be possible. I knew a great deal about the colonial policy of European powers and I felt sure that such a trip would be plain idiotic.

I knew that American Negroes or even Negroes from the colonies who had European contact were not desired in the colonies and for an American Negro to travel in the colonies with a white woman was not to be thought of.

When I found that she was serious I voiced my opinions on these matters, but she dismissed them all. I told her, how-

ever, that I would consider going on the trip only if she took
a white man along also. This she finally consented to do.

So, while in London she proposed to Otto Theis, an
American journalist and a good friend of us both, that he
come to Africa with us.

His answers were always very non-committal but
Nancy considered them to be in the affirmative.

Later Otto told me that he could not go; that although
the six months away would cost him nothing, he would also
be making nothing. Nancy's idea was that Otto could probably collect material that would be of some use to him later
in a literary way.

When I informed her that Otto had decided against her
proposition she angrily told me that I was to blame for his
refusal.

Why she should charge me with this was incomprehen-
sible. Otto's reasons were perfectly rational. To take a six
months' trip away, lose touch with what interests he had and
return without any financial gain was to him a foolish thing
to do. So the proposition fell through.

This plan to go to Africa was discussed pro and con
between Nancy and myself on many occasions and though
she persisted in stating her desire to go there with me I knew
full well that I would never go.

While we were there the friendship between Nancy and
Bimbo continued to grow. Nancy also received letters regularly from Bob Scanlon who had returned to Paris.

Also during the time we were in London Nancy and I
spent a great deal of time with Wyn Henderson, the woman
who was engaged in the publishing business, and a man who
assisted her by the name of John Sibthorpe.

Nancy and Wyn became fast friends and I also enjoyed
a great many pleasant hours with John. But despite her
friendship with Wyn, Nancy was also spending a great deal
of time with Bimbo.

So much was she taken up with Bimbo that the two left

London for some nearby provincial village to spend a few days alone together. Although they seemed happy enough before they left I think this trip was fatal to their friendship.

While they were away I received a letter that nearly jarred me out of my senses. Or maybe it would be more correct to say it jarred me into my senses. It was from my wife. And to make the jar a little harder she sent along a large photograph.

She could not have timed their arrival better had she known the exact circumstances under which I was living then. With Nancy away in the country with Bimbo I had begun to feel very melancholy and lonely. I felt as though I had been abandoned and—not for another man but for another woman.

When the photograph arrived with news from my wife I immediately decided to leave everything and return to America. I did not care then how much pain extracting the foot was going to cause; I was going. I showed the picture to Wyn Henderson and she also advised me to return. That settled it.

I went out and cabled my wife that I was coming home. Little did I know, however, that much was to happen before I was to eventually get back to America.

When Nancy and Bimbo returned to London I informed Nancy of my determination to return to America. After a long discussion she approved of my making the trip but asked me to make two promises. One was that I buy a round trip passage ticket when I sailed and the other was that I first return to Paris with her. I agreed. As a result, my sailing was postponed indefinitely.

At this time Nancy also asked me about taking John and Wyn back to Paris with us to manage the press. I thought it an excellent idea as I knew Nancy was becoming tired of her little private printing business and wanted to be free herself.

When asked, they consented so the four of us left with Bimbo for Paris. The days following our return were filled with excitement.

Norman Douglas, the writer, arrived from Venice on one of his periodic trips to see his dentist. As he was counted among Nancy's best friends he was her guest. Harold Acton, also a writer, was in Paris and frequently in the company of Douglas with us.

Douglas is an intensely interesting person and it amused me to see the lesser English and American literary personages in Paris fall all over themselves to get in his company.

He was always in a cheerful mood and inseparable from his snuff which he insisted on making everyone in his party try. Once was enough for me and although he always tried to get me to have another sniff I always firmly refused.

Nancy's plan to take a trip to Africa was proposed to him while he was there and he tentatively accepted the invitation. Later he and I had lunch together and he told me he could not go to Africa and that I was to tell Nancy as much.

This I refused to do because I remembered the unhappy results of telling her that Otto Theis had refused to go. Douglas later wrote to her giving his reasons for not going, one of which included the mountainous seas of the Bay of Biscay and what he said was the reputed inefficiency of sailors.

This letter gave Nancy no little disappointment but Douglas is still one of the few old friends with whom Nancy is still in communication.

Also during the time we spent in Paris Nancy became acquainted with a young French boy under 20 years of age who had run away from his home and school. His name was Raymond Michelet. When Nancy met him he was a fugitive from his father, an ex–police official. I was told the father was determined to find the boy and was looking in every likely place he thought the lad might be.

The boy, who was hiding here and there with the father close on his heels, was in imminent danger of being captured.

In her typical fashion, Nancy took him, and as his protector, whisked him away to the country. Once there she set about making herself his mistress, a thing she accomplished with a certain degree of success I believe.

The first time I saw the lad was when Nancy brought him down to Chapelle-Réanville. One could see youthful innocence and inexperience all over his face. He was rather shy and very quiet.

On his first night there Nancy was busy showing him some pictures in a large book in the hall. I sat near the fire reading, now and then casually glancing in their direction.

I noticed that Nancy was making a quiet but determined effort to get as close as possible to the boy. Of course, from former experience, I knew immediately what was in the wind. If Nancy succeeded the lad would not be so innocent in the morning.

After a time Nancy became conscious of the fact that I was watching her. Immediately I was told she desired to be alone with her guest.

I retired to my room to my books and liquor. Shortly afterwards, I heard the boy climb the stairs and by the sound of his feet on the steps I was given the impression that he was displeased about something.

I wondered what had happened. Soon afterwards Nancy came through my room going to her own. I asked her if anything was wrong.

"Oh, no," she replied, "the boy seems a little bashful, that's all."

I did not see much of Raymond after this first meeting but he was involved in my affairs for the following two years or so.

CHAPTER X

Flawed Efforts

THE FIRST RESOLUTION I had made in London to immediately return home turned out to be one of those "tomorrow" affairs. In Paris, when I again spoke to Nancy about my returning to America, she always asked me to postpone my departure. In every case, I finally consented.

The press was then in the hands of Wyn Henderson and that gave Nancy more free time. So the question of my sailing was rather indefinite. I had not dropped my plans to return home but I am afraid they were not foremost in my mind during those days.

Finally, when it appeared as though I really was going to get away, Nancy proposed that we make another trip to the South of France. As I had not seen much of the country before and loved it, I did not want to pass up the chance of visiting it again.

So all of the necessary luggage was packed into the rumble seat of the car and off we went. As a whole it was a very delightful trip. We went through south-west France in leisurely stages almost to the Spanish frontier, and then over some of the lower ranges of the Pyrenees. We were looking for a likely place to spend the summer.

As nothing suitable was found Nancy decided that we should go northward to the Dordogne River. The days were hot and the mountain driving tedious. There were outbursts of temper from both of us. A tiny little village near the Dordogne itself called Creysse was finally selected.

There happened to be a two room furnished hut in the

village that had not been occupied for some years that was available. We took it.

The floors were scrubbed, windows washed, a new outhouse built in the back yard, a piano rented, a supply of liquor put in and we settled down for the summer.

The village was charming and despite its lack of modern conveniences I enjoyed the stay in its peaceful atmosphere. The river was the only place to bathe. Water had to be brought from the village well and the worst food I ever ate in my life was served to us from the local restaurant.

With the aid of many Pernods I completed the composition of a book of songs I was writing and we spent a very pleasant time in the place. Yet, as the summer progressed, I realized more and more that Nancy and I would never get along together.

The constant clash in temperaments, the frequent harsh words we exchanged over mere nothings presaged trouble in the future and too my memory was pregnant with thoughts of what had happened in the past.

We left Creysse and motored towards the Riviera, stopping at Marseilles and Toulon. In Toulon we discovered Princess Murat. The day we met her she was in a very agitated condition. I did not know what was wrong with her. I have seen the Princess since then and before that meeting but never as she appeared when we found her in Toulon.

She is a very charming woman and I like her very much. While there I had the very pleasant job of using my car to move her belongings from one hotel to another. I never discovered the reason why she moved.

I shall always remember the grace and dignity with which she could smoke "the pipe." It is truly a work of art. But she is lovely and an extraordinary charming hostess. She is an intense admirer of Louis Armstrong and has a great number of his records.

Probably the most pleasant two hours of my life in Europe were spent aboard her yacht in the harbor at Toulon. Nancy was of course with me during all of this time.

Leaving Toulon, we went further along the coast to-

Cover of Henry-Music, *showing Henry with Nancy's bracelet-encased arms on his shoulders. Photomontage by Man Ray, courtesy Anne Chisholm.*

wards Italy, finally settling in a small sea-coast town a few miles from there.

It was now late in the fall. The place was practically deserted and the "mistral," the north winds which come down the Rhone Valley, was making itself evident. We walked and motored about the countryside.

It was during the stay there that Nancy told me of her idea of writing and publishing the Negro anthology. She had mentioned doing such a work before but I had never taken her announcements very seriously. I had never encouraged her greatly, for knowing her as I did, I hardly thought her the right person to produce such a work and obtain the best results.

This time, she talked so many hours about it I was firmly convinced that she meant to carry it through. I told her it was a splendid idea but that it was an extremely difficult job to attempt. But she was not to be deterred; she told me of her plans and of the people she thought of asking to contribute to the book.

The Negroes she mentioned at first were nobodies in so far as they represented true Negro progress. I argued that to make her book worthwhile she must get contributions from colored people who had accomplished something of real worth and had done outstanding work in the advancement of their race.

Among the men I mentioned at that time were included such persons as Walter White, W. E. B. DuBois, William Pickens and Dr. Adams, Dean of Howard University Medical School, as well as a number of noted musicians and writers whom I knew personally.

Nancy eventually did contact a great number of these Negro leaders and got articles for her book. She also saw quite a few personally on her second trip to America. But the Negroes she met personally in Europe who wrote for the book with a few exceptions such as Eric Waldron, Clarence White, the well-known Negro violinist, and possibly one or two theatrical celebrities, they were not persons whom I would choose to present as representatives of the progress made by the Negroes.

An example of this was the contribution she secured from boxers. I could see no purpose in wasting space on the life stories of these persons.

I continually advised her that it was absolutely necessary

that the very best Negro achievement should be included in the book. To tell the plain truth, I did not think that she was a person who was capable of doing the work she proposed to me at that time.

Later, after I had read the results of her tremendous efforts I was and still am of the opinion that Nancy Cunard bit off more than she could chew in attempting to edit this Negro anthology. I was thoroughly familiar with the compilation of a great deal of it and even while giving full credit for the great amount of work and terrific expense connected with the book I do think it could have been greatly improved had its production been in other hands.

First of all, Nancy was woefully uninformed on the subject. She knew very little about Negroes then. She knows more now but at that time they were more or less alike to her and most of the few she knew were of the lower class.

However, she did attain a remarkable degree of success in doing the book and I was frankly astonished at the result obtained. She dedicated the book to me and I have a measure of pride in this fact but I must admit that I think the book has many very glaring faults, some of which I consider pitiful. Other mistakes might be described as downright idiotic and sheer nonsense.

Hundreds of dollars were wasted on the compilation of the anthology. A great deal of material was put into the book that meant absolutely nothing. Then again, as always, Nancy injected her personal feelings and leanings in the work to the extent of being what I consider rude to say the least.

She asked Dr. DuBois, the world known Negro leader, to write an article for her. He consented, but I do not think he wrote a new piece for her, telling Nancy to use something of his that had been printed previously.

She did use an article of his in the book but followed it by a severe criticism of him and his political leanings and the attitude he took in his writings. I felt this very much because I had introduced her to Dr. DuBois and greatly admired him as a former instructor of mine at Atlanta University.

I remember asking her why she had done this. Nancy replied:

"Because I felt it was necessary and proper."

I thought it was damned bad taste.

She also had hard things to say of all Negroes who failed or refused to contribute, notably Eric Waldron and Countee Cullen.

The production is an extraordinary example of persistence in the face of tremendous odds, the greatest of which was ignorance. Nancy made up her mind to do it and she did.

The book to my way of thinking does not justify the effort put into the making of it for the very good reason that she did not know what she was doing.

The cost was tremendous and Nancy often voiced her disappointment at the small sales and what she said she considered the lack of appreciation from Negroes of her effort to espouse their achievements. The thought and plan were brilliant, but they were very badly executed.

While we were on the Riviera at this time the fires of hatred Nancy nursed for her mother burst into a great flame. At some time previous Lady Cunard had informed Nancy that her regular allowance would be reduced. The reason given was heavy income-taxes. Nancy was very suspicious of this excuse.

The fact was that Nancy had worked herself into such a rage against her mother that she said she did not want any more money from Her Ladyship anyway. Nancy would say some awful things about Lady Cunard when in these moods.

I never really agreed with Nancy in her attitude toward her mother. I could never understand how anyone could feel as she did toward her own mother. I often asked her not to discuss Her Ladyship in my presence. Once Nancy wrote a very nasty letter to her mother about the allowance incident and read it to me before posting it. I remember she gave me the letter to mail but I destroyed it instead. Nancy never knew.

Subsequently Nancy wrote the "Blackman and Her Ladyship" pamphlet which she had printed and distributed herself. I thought it a most idiotic thing to do. I received a copy while in America. Why she ever wrote that atrocious piece is more than I know.

About this time Nancy received news that George Moore, the famous novelist, had decided to delete her from his will. George Moore was a great friend of Nancy's mother. The evident reason for the rumored deletion was because of reports that Nancy had a Negro lover.

Nancy immediately wrote to Mr. Moore to ascertain the facts. Not because she was seriously concerned about what Moore would leave her, but because she had her own ideas about why he was reported to have done it. His reply was that he had in no way made any change in his will. What this meant I did not know but I don't think Nancy received any legacy from his estate upon his death.

During this trip south trouble also arose at the press. Wyn Henderson was making a mess of everything as far as we could learn. Richard Aldington, who seemed to know something of Wyn's past record, raised the very devil when he learned that she was handling one of his books.

The outcome of this was a break between Nancy and Aldington. More difficulties arose with a book by Laura Riding. There were also complications over the book by the American writer, Ezra Pound, "XXX Cantos." With all of these troubles Nancy became tired of the whole business and decided to close the shop, so after our return to Paris a few weeks later the Hours Press ceased to exist.

I was sorry about all of these misunderstandings. I had known Pound for some time. I remember that Pound also laid claim to having musical abilities for I once took some of his manuscripts to arrange them for the piano. But I also recall that I could not understand any of them. I have been in his company many times in London and in Paris. We celebrated our first meeting in a café-restaurant in Paris by joyfully singing "Roll Jordan, Roll" which I must admit he sings very well.

When we heard that so much trouble had arisen we

decided to return to Paris. I was glad for the trip had done neither of us any good. Contrary to what one would expect, my health was in a very bad state and Nancy was on the verge of a collapse.

Winter was at hand and the press was closed. Nancy was at a loose end. She wanted activity but she was not certain what to do. For myself, I made no attempt to find a job as I had clung to the intention of returning to America.

Nothing seemed settled and I was again thinking about sailing when Nancy suddenly asked me if I would like to visit the Austrian Alps with her for the winter sports. It seems that on our last trip to London she had received an invitation from Brian Howard, a young English poet, to visit him at Ober-Gurgl that winter.

Although I had met Brian in London and had found him to be a very likeable chap, I was not too anxious to make the trip. I knew if I consented it would be months before I would ever get to America and besides, Brian, so far as I could learn, seemingly preferred the company of men to that of women.

Probably he was an excellent poet. On that score I certainly can't act as critic but according to what Nancy told me he derived most of his income from his American mother.

I told Nancy of my objections but she finally persuaded me to accompany her. A few speedy days followed in which skiing equipment was bought, a day set for the departure and we packed for an extended trip.

CHAPTER XI

Austrian Scenes

I HAVE OFTEN BEEN TOLD that Nancy used dope. I have always refuted this statement because I have never seen her use any. But on two occasions I have very strongly suspected her of having taken some sort of drug.

On the night before we were to leave for Ober-Gurgl Nancy disappeared. Just where she went I never knew but the next day about half an hour before train time she turned up at the hotel in a terrible state. That morning was one of the times I strongly believed Nancy was under the influence of drugs.

She was in a perfectly drunken condition. After considerable fuss and bustle the luggage was bundled into a taxi and off we went to the station. I am sure she had no realization of what was happening.

Owing to the excitement and rush of leaving we overlooked one of my handbags and Nancy's typewriter.

We were finally safely in the train, however, and Nancy immediately climbed into her berth fully clothed and lapsed into unconsciousness. Just before she fell asleep she gave me explicit instructions to rouse her for dinner. It was about mid-day at that time.

She slept through the entire afternoon. About seven o'clock I called her for dinner. It was with the utmost difficulty that I succeeded in getting her partly awake. A scene followed.

"What the hell do you want? Why don't you leave me alone?" she demanded of me in her stupor.

"But you told me to get you up for dinner," I replied.

"No, damn it, go away," she commanded.

"You told me to get you up and up you are coming," I said, at the same time practically pulling her out of the berth.

"You are a damned fool. You won't let well enough alone. Go away," she insisted.

But I did not. I stayed right there for I was determined that she get up. We had nearly missed the train because of her; she had slept the entire afternoon. I was in no mood for arguing so my persistence finally succeeded.

Reeling and rocking, half awake and still in a stupor, she followed me to the dining-car. When seated her head started dropping and she was alternately awake and asleep. Dinner was served but she ate practically nothing. Finally coffee.

At this time a very attractive looking Englishman sitting almost opposite signified that he would like to speak to me.

I went over to him. He said he was a newspaper correspondent on his way to Vienna and asked if the lady with me was Nancy Cunard. I replied in the affirmative. He immediately expressed a great desire to meet her so I undertook to introduce him.

He came to our table. After getting a semblance of sense in Nancy's beclouded brain I said:

"Nancy, this is Mr. Roy Randall of London and Vienna who desires to meet you."

She sleepily acknowledged the introduction and he tried to keep up a conversation. Nancy's replies came between nods and winks. I succeeded in keeping her partly awake by kicking her foot underneath the table. Randall did not seem the least disconcerted by her condition.

Soon, to my great relief, Nancy began to show signs of a returning intelligence and in a few moments she and Randall were engaged in an animated conversation.

The dinner finished well with liquors and smokes. But I was tired. I suggested to Nancy that we had better get some sleep.

To my surprise she invited Randall to join us in the sleeping compartment for more drinks and along he came.

When we arrived she again climbed into her berth fully dressed and after a few moments of conversation, fell asleep.

Randall lingered on to my great disgust for as long as he remained I could not go to bed. At last he decided to go. It was necessary to wake Nancy again so he could say good night. When he stood up his head came about on a level with the upper berth in which Nancy had been sleeping.

She raised her body slightly, looked at him a moment; then impulsively threw her arms around his neck and kissed him passionately. He returned the embrace with equal fervor.

What did I think of all this? I sat calmly looking on. I had ceased to be surprised at anything Nancy did; I had come to a point where I realized that those spontaneous shows of emotion were a part of her. By accepting Nancy, I also accepted them. Randall left a few moments later and I went to bed.

I awoke next morning to find Nancy missing. Wondering, I dressed and sauntered off to breakfast. There, in the diner sat Nancy and Randall, talking very cheerily over a finished meal. I very politely said good-morning, took a table and proceeded to eat alone.

For the remainder of the trip Nancy and Randall got along famously. By the time we reached our destination late that afternoon a great friendship had seemingly sprung up between them. She promised to visit him in Vienna later.

Poor Randall, he little knew what he was letting himself in for. But it was his affair so I kept my mouth shut. We left him in the train to continue his journey to Vienna.

During the day on the train there was another scene between Nancy and myself. It came about when we discovered the bag and the typewriter had been left behind. She flew into a terrible rage and looking at me as though I was an arch-criminal exploded with this:

"I'll make you pay for this and pay dearly!"

"You should have come to the hotel in a sensible condition and maybe nothing would have gone wrong," was my only reply.

This anger toward me was still raging when we left the train. I was indifferent to everything by that time. The type-writer, my bag and her. None of them meant anything to me. From the very beginning the trip had been a headache for me. Many times that day I wished I had stuck to my intention of returning to America.

After our waiting a few hours at the station, Brian How-ard arrived and we boarded a bus for the second stage of the journey to Ober-Gurgl. We arrived at the end of the bus route about seven o'clock. It was clear and cold.

We took some warm drinks and the decision was made to move on up the mountain in sleighs. I was positively opposed to the move, stating that it was better to remain where we were for the night and continue in the morning.

I was over-ruled so we packed ourselves into three sleighs and started up the highest, roughest, and coldest part of the journey.

The trip was long and it got colder every minute. Nancy who naturally suffers from cold, was having a hell of a bad time. She imagined at one time that she was freezing to death. She refused to ride further and got off her sleigh to walk.

She later told me that she seriously contemplated suicide during the journey. For the entire latter part of the trip she was in a perfect rage, finally turning on poor Brian for ever proposing that we visit him.

Brian took it all philosophically and of course I said nothing. I knew if I opened my mouth hell really would break loose.

At last in the hotel, we gradually thawed out with the aid of hot drinks, and were assigned rooms. Here again difficulties arose. The main hotel was full so we were com-pelled to take rooms in the annex next door.

The country for miles around was covered with snow but the weather was warm and sunny until about three in the afternoon. From three o'clock on it would suddenly turn cold and by night the thermometer always fell close to zero.

Skiing was the principal outdoor pastime. Brian was

Brian Howard, Nancy Cunard, Henry Crowder and two friends in Austria, 1931. Photo courtesy Anne Chisholm.

very efficient at this but Nancy made one effort and promptly quit. For a novice and a beginner I did pretty well.

During all of this time we were both ill. Nancy suffered more than I. The lack of proper heat in the rooms and the inconvenience of bathing facilities did not contribute to Nancy's peace of mind.

Brian was having difficulties with his boy friend because

of another male rival. Nancy seemed to have a special attachment for Brian so some interesting episodes followed.

For one thing, Brian got into a terrible state. There were
quarrels, arguments and even tears. One night five of us,
Nancy, myself, Brian, his boy friend and his rival, went to a
fete dance. There was a scene.

Brian's rival took possession of his boy friend and Brian
would not stand for it. Nancy, in some manner, got herself
mixed up in the quarrel because she was all for Brian.

Some very sharp recriminations followed; the boy friend
got fed up and decided to go back to the hotel. I had also
noticed resentment in Nancy rising against me—it always did
when she became intoxicated—because she wanted to be left
alone with Brian. So I also decided it was time for me to
leave. Accordingly the boy friend and I walked away from
the place followed by some very uncomplimentary shouts
from our erstwhile companions.

At our hotel we separated. He went to the main building
and I went to my room in the annex. Hours later Nancy and
Brian returned. It seemed that Brian had experienced difficulty in getting into his room and had come along with
Nancy to talk over the situation.

I heard this long discussion from my room as it was next
to Nancy's. She was trying to persuade him to remain in her
room all night. He was steadfastly refusing to do so. The talk
went on but Nancy did not seem to be making much progress.

She then locked the door to prevent his leaving. Brian
thereupon opened the communicating door leading into my
room, came in, opened the window, stepped out into the
snow, and was gone.

It all happened so quickly that it was over before I realized what was taking place. No sooner had he stepped out
of the window than Nancy entered and began to question me
in a hysterical voice.

"Where is Brian?" she demanded.

"I don't know, he just went out of the window," I replied
from the covers of my bed.

"What! You fool! Why did you let him go?" she demanded, raising her voice.

"I could not stop him," I said, adding, "Why should I? He wanted to go and he went."

"Damn you," she said. "If Brian kills himself you will be to blame for it."

"Me to blame," I answered, "what the devil have I got to do with it if Brian kills himself?"

"Because," she tried to reason, "that is what he is going to do and I was trying to keep him here to prevent it. And you, fool that you are, let him get out."

My reaction to this outburst was an absolute blank. I turned over and proceeded to go to sleep to the accompaniment of her sobs next door. Nothing came of the supposed suicide attempt but the situation became more tense and conditions were disagreeable on every side.

The end was reached one night when a particularly nasty scene occurred in my room. Nancy, being very drunk, returned to her room, took up a shoe, and broke every windowpane in the place. She seemed to have forgotten that the weather outside was sub-zero.

And the peculiar part about it was that the windows were all double glassed and made of many small squares. Nevertheless, she very carefully smashed each and every one of them. I offered no interference.

The next day when the astonished manager made inquiry Nancy's only comment was to ask for the cost of the damages done.

Then followed arguments with the bar maid over the serving and cost of drinks in the wine room; quarrels about Nancy's room. Her physical condition became worse. Her nerves were shattered.

A series of telegrams to and from Roy Randall in Vienna followed. Shortly afterwards—to my great relief and I am sure to that of the manager's also—we checked out of Ober-Gurgl and some 24 hours later were met in Vienna by Randall. He took us to his rather luxurious flat.

Some strange things happened there. I am sure the landlady did not relish our coming and I think objected particularly to me. But we remained.

Randall very graciously gave up his bedroom to us. It
contained twin beds. He slept on a big divan in the next room.

We were only in Vienna for a few days but in that time
we did a lot. The opera, a Strauss concert, some sightseeing
and a little shopping.

Nancy's health seemed to improve and her nerves
seemed quieter. For that I was glad.

I particularly recall the night after the Strauss concert
when the three of us had a late supper together. The color
question came up and Randall displayed such ignorance on
the subject that Nancy left the restaurant in a very angry
mood.

Randall and I remained where we were, quietly continuing our conversation and presently Nancy returned. Peace
was restored so we all returned to the apartment.

Drinks were served and desultory conversation continued for some time. For some reason Randall left the room
for a moment and Nancy quickly turned to me saying:

"I want to be alone with our host for a while."

Knowing this was an invitation for me to leave, I went
in the next room and went to bed.

Nancy came into the room the next morning after day-
light and crawled into her bed.

On another night shortly before leaving she and our host
became so amorous in my presence that I went to bed without
being asked. Again she remained in the next room with Randall all night.

Those events caused me no concern. I was only passing
the time away until I was to return to the United States. I
knew that that was now close to hand for I was thoroughly
disgusted and wanted to leave at the earliest possible chance.

Two days later we left Vienna for Paris where I quickly
got my things together, packed and set a date for sailing. I
was sure nothing was going to prevent me from leaving. The

trip had already been postponed again and again, and each time I had been sorry I had changed my mind.

So I was off on the first trip I had made to America since I first sailed down the Hudson so filled with hopes, desires, ambitions and stern resolutions. The hopes had not been realized; the desires had not been answered; the ambitions had not been attained and the resolutions had been forgotten. Nancy came to the station to see me off. Among her last words were: "Remember you have promised to come back." I did not realize then that before the year was to close I was destined to make this westward journey two more times. And all because of Nancy.

CHAPTER XII

Visits to America

M Y FIRST TRIP to America was not particularly eventful. I had my return ticket in my pocket but no date had been set for my return sailing. I was to inform Nancy when I intended coming back to France.

But I did look forward to seeing my own country again after an absence of over 18 months. As I lolled in a deck chair on the way over I wondered just how changed things would seem to me. I knew the country itself could not have changed much in that length of time but I knew I was going back possessing many new aspects on life itself.

I felt I had experienced all of the freedom a man of my race had ever known. I had lived most of the time in a country where no color bar existed. I had been as free as a black man could be. Had all of this changed me to such an extent I could never again live happily in my own country?

No. Color bar or no color bar I felt as much at home when I arrived in Harlem as if I had never left. Its crowded, busy streets seemed the same as ever; my old friends seemed the same; nothing seemed changed. I found that instead of changing my views of life had only broadened. I saw much of it in a new light but in a much fuller one.

On to Washington. I arrived there with mixed feelings. I had not heard from my wife since the letter I received in London. I was not sure where she was, what she was doing or how she felt about me. I wanted to know all of those things.

When I did locate her one of the first things she asked about was my relations with Nancy. She had heard many stories, she said, about my living with a wealthy white woman. She wanted to know if they were true.

I evaded none of her questions. I answered them all. I began with Venice and told her the complete story. I told her why I had not written to her—because many of my letters had gone unanswered and I thought she was interested in someone else. She did little to rectify the impression I had gained from her silence. And in sharp, cutting words I was told that I was not the kind of husband I should be.

That ended the matter. We were still more than friends but certainly not man and wife again. After our first meeting she seemed not the least interested in what I did or where I went. I saw her on a number of occasions but that was all. Not once did we ever discuss living together again. She was evidently satisfied with her life and was only too willing to let me live mine as I saw fit. That satisfied me.

I stayed in America about two months and a half. I took a much needed breathing spell from the tense atmosphere Nancy always seemed to surround herself with. I enjoyed the stay and felt much better upon returning to Europe for not only had my wife and I come to an understanding but I felt much better physically.

It was late spring when I arrived in Paris and discovered that Nancy was in Cagnes, on the Riviera near Nice. She had left money to cover my expenses down to Toulon where I was to meet her but I hesitated about taking it.

The question again arose whether I wanted to continue the affair. What had I gained and where had it gotten me were some of the thoughts that ran through my mind.

I had gone to America and come back at her expense. I felt I owed her something more than a thank you and a good-bye when I returned. She wanted me to meet her in Toulon. I went.

We stayed the first night there together and the next day went to Cagnes. When we got there Nancy informed me that she had taken a small house and was living with Raymond, the young French boy whom she had helped to hide from his father. I was told to find myself a room at a hotel on the

sea-front. She also informed me that it would be better if I
did not call at the house as Raymond might not understand.

I readily fell in with the idea so when we met it was in
my hotel.

Eric Waldron, the talented Negro writer, whom we had
met sometime previously in Toulon and whom we later saw
in Bandol, came to visit us in Cagnes. Nancy seemed very
much interested in Eric. He went to her house to dine but
without my accompanying him.

After being in Cagnes for a few days and motoring
about the surrounding country, I asked Nancy what her plans
were for the summer.

"You might go on into Italy, take a house there, get a
piano and practice," she said, "I intend to go into the mountains with Raymond."

"Nothing doing," was all this sudden revelation of her
intentions brought from me. "Stay with Raymond if you
desire," I continued, "but I am going back to Paris."

Just back from America without a plan of my own; on
the Riviera at her request and to be told that I could go into
Italy "somewhere" for the summer was a little more than I
could swallow.

I had received an invitation to attend an international
weekend party in London which was sponsored by a Miss
Koutane so I decided to go to that. Nancy and I discussed the
entire situation but could come to no mutual agreement so I
started back north.

While in Cagnes Nancy had met a Negro painter whom
I later learned was successful in either borrowing or being
given a thousand francs. He is now a teacher in an important
Negro University in Atlanta, Georgia. I saw him while in
Cagnes but knew nothing then of the real relations which
existed between the two.

On my way to Paris I stopped in Bandol for 10 days and
lived in the same house with Eric Waldron who was staying
in the town at the time. We spent some very pleasant hours
together.

While still there I decided to return to America after my trip to London. I wanted to say good-bye to the whole affair. At no time during all of our relations had I felt so determined to cut loose from everything and return to America for good. I had only been in France one month.

I informed Nancy of my intention by letter. Some rapid fire correspondence followed between us which ended by the startling announcement that Nancy wanted to go to America with me. She had already decided to meet me in Paris after my return from London.

I can't describe the effect this decision of hers had on me. I had been surprised at many things Nancy had done but never had I even guessed she would want to do such a foolhardy thing.

Imagine, a Negro man sailing into New York in the company of a wealthy white woman. I couldn't. To make matters worse Nancy was the kind who would want to go everywhere and see everything. Had she been willing to go alone that would have been alright but I knew she would want me to go with her.

To say her announcement stunned me would be putting it much too mildly. First of all she had told me her plans for the summer and that was my main reason for returning to America. She was seemingly infatuated with the young French boy and I thought it best to clear out.

This sudden decision of hers bothered me to no end. But I again thought of the future. Fool that I was, I reasoned that the trip might change her and I might yet build on what looked like the ruins of our association.

So according to her directions I booked passages for both of us on a German boat sailing early in July when I reached Paris.

After a pleasant weekend in England I returned to Paris to meet Nancy who was all prepared for the crossing. We journeyed to Cherbourg and I boarded the steamer full of forebodings.

The trip was disagreeable from the very start because

Nancy was a poor sailor and though not really ill she stuck to her cabin most of the time. She would have her meals with me excepting breakfast which she always took in bed.

Occasionally she would take a walk around the deck but she was pretty miserable as she was longing for Raymond. Almost daily she sent radio messages to him from the boat.

But I could not be bothered about all of that as I had plenty of my own troubles. My mind was occupied with thoughts of the possible consequences of our arrival in New York together.

I pondered deeply over what was going to happen. I visualized all sorts of complications. What would we do? Where could we go? Where would she stay, and in general, what was actually going to happen?

Although I had come to an understanding with my wife I was not sure what she might do if she learned that I was in New York with Nancy. I saw trouble from every quarter. Frankly, I was scared. But the die was then cast and there was no turning back.

I played and sang a great deal on this trip to help me forget my troubles. All of my fellow passengers were very nice but I worried more and more as we neared the American coast. On the whole I was full of worries but one incident which happened about four days out from France relieved my mind a bit.

I was sitting in the writing room one afternoon finishing some letters when a young German woman who was sitting opposite me dropped a tightly folded note in front of me.

I took it up and glanced at the sender. Upon opening it I read that the writer desired to talk to me but as her husband was aboard she asked if I would consent to meet her in another class of the boat.

After thinking the matter over for a moment I decided in the negative. On the back of the note which she asked to be returned to her, I wrote that if she desired to talk to me she would have to do so in the class in which we were travelling—tourist class.

It was arranged that we meet on the saloon deck outside of the smoking room. We met and talked. She told me of her early life, of her education in a convent, of the efforts of the priest who was her teacher to seduce her and how she had finally returned to her parents.

She said that she had always been told that Negroes were dirty, diseased and to be avoided, but for some reason she was attracted to me and wanted to know me.

She was afraid of what her husband would say if he caught her talking to me so that was the reason she had proposed we meet in another class of the boat. I set her at ease on this question by telling her that black men were not different from other people except in color; that aboard ship it was usual for passengers to converse with one another regardless of race.

The sequel of this meeting, of which Nancy knew nothing, was that the girl fell madly in love with me and told me she would like to be my wife. I have a photograph of her and a generous lock of her hair besides many letters as remembrances of this meeting.

On arrival in America she went on to Albany and wrote me of her desire to meet me in New York City. But because I was so fully occupied with steering Nancy around I did not answer her letters and never saw her again.

As we docked my fears of what might happen rose to a frenzy almost. I thought of myself, a poor Georgia black man, going through the United States Customs with a reputedly wealthy English white woman. I shuddered. But we got through without any trouble.

I gave a sigh of relief and headed straight for Harlem where I had decided I was going to take Nancy long before the ship docked. I knew if she would stay there with me a lot of trouble would be avoided. I had also made up my mind that I was not going to stay anywhere else with her.

We first went to a hotel on 135th Street between Seventh and Eighth Avenue. After battling with the bed-bugs there for two nights we secured other quarters in the Grampion

Hotel which figured so prominently in the many newspaper articles about Nancy on her subsequent trip to America.

During the short time we were in New York I was in a constant turmoil. Nancy, as I had imagined, wanted to go everywhere and see everything there was to see. I could not make her understand that New York was not Paris. She proposed doing many, many things that I knew could not be done.

There were many examples of this. On one occasion she demanded that I go into a very expensive ice cream salon on lower Fifth Avenue with her.

"You go on in," I said, "I'll be waiting on the corner for you when you come out." She never went in but she was very mad because I would not accompany her. But I did not dare. I knew I would never be served if I sat down at a table.

At another time after we had been to see Marc Connelly's play, "Green Pastures," she wanted to stroll along Broadway in the downtown theatrical district which was crowded with after-theater-goers.

I knew it was too risky to try and refused to go. I knew I would not get twenty steps before a white man would "accidentally" bump into me, a fight would follow and then where would I be? Anyone who has lived in New York knows the answer.

In that case Nancy persisted. We started quarrelling on the corner and our voices were raised to such an extent that we began to attract attention. It looked like a tight place for me but she finally consented to get in a cab with me and we drove off.

I had to continually keep telling her that we could not do things in America as we had done them in France. There was much unpleasantness and continuous quarrels. As the days passed we both became increasingly bad tempered.

One day she induced me to take her to the Aquarium which is down on the point where the Hudson and East rivers flow into the bay. There is a large park around the building which is frequented by the poorer classes of lower New York and the East Side.

Nancy wanted to walk through the park with me and suggested that we sit on the grass for a rest. It was no pleasant job for me to have to refuse and she took my excuses in such a way that it made me the more miserable.

Every day something came up to make me wish Nancy had never come to New York and I am sure she felt the same way in many instances.

One afternoon when we were walking down Riverside Drive near 155th Street, a car containing two white men passed us. One of them yelled at Nancy:

"Why don't you take a white man?"

She asked me why didn't I do something about it. What could I do or say? I had to "take it" and like it. Everywhere we went we were stared at very belligerently and I became more and more uncomfortable.

On her part Nancy was always complaining about the heat. She declared that she hated America and wanted to get away as soon as possible.

To make matters worse for me I was nervous about my wife. Everyone in Harlem knew her and I knew it would only be a matter of days until she learned that I was there with Nancy. I knew if she did decide to do something there would be hell to pay. God, how I hated myself for ever saying I would visit New York with Nancy.

Me, of all people, a great big black man, running around New York with a white woman. I must have been crazy.

We spent one very pleasant evening when we visited some white friends of Nancy's in New Jersey and another weekend in a charming cottage a few miles from New York that was owned by a Negro-Indian couple. But outside of that tempers and feelings were usually at the boiling point.

I introduced Nancy to the personnel of *The Crisis,* the magazine published by Negroes. She met Walter White, DuBois, and William Pickens.

Pickens escorted us on a short tour through Harlem and
introduced Nancy to various people but she was not too well
received. She was white, they were black; they could not
forget the difference.

Some of the prominent Negroes, however, were very
interested in meeting Nancy and to know of her interest in
Negro affairs. I think she received contributions from all of
them for her Negro anthology. Walter White proposed some
sort of party for her but it never materialized.

One night, when we were liquored-up on moonshine
we took a flying trip to Washington, D.C. I must have been
crazy that night for I sure was skating on thin ice by going
into the same town where my wife lived. What a scene could
have taken place had she known! A funny feeling runs down
my back now when I think about what might have happened.

During all of these days, we were drinking plenty of
moonshine and Nancy was fretting about being away from
Raymond. The situation became more and more tense. We
quarrelled a lot. I finally became so enraged I demanded:

"Why don't you return to France and your Raymond?"

"I will do so," she replied instantly.

Sailing schedules were examined and return reservations
made for two weeks later. The following day, however,
another quarrel occurred which resulted in the cancellation of
the former reservations and a boat sailing in about four days
was selected.

After a very drunken party to which we were invited
on the night of our departure, we clambered aboard a German
steamer and headed back for Europe.

As I was practically unconscious from the moonshine,
I did not remember any of the details of the departure. When
I awoke we were miles out at sea.

Thinking back on it, that stay in New York was one of
the most unpleasant incidents in my life. No one can imagine
how glad I was when I awoke and found myself aboard that
steamer. It all seemed like a dream but a bad one where green

devils jump all over the bed and jab you with three-pronged forks. I hope I never have such an experience again.

And I am sure the visit was just as miserable for Nancy as it was for me. I could never imagine why she ever made up her mind to go. Every moment of her time was filled with longing for Raymond.

The return trip to Europe was uneventful. I amused myself in various ways but Nancy was so concerned about Raymond that she spent a great deal of her time in her cabin. As on the trip over, she sent him wireless messages almost every day.

As the ship neared Europe we agreed that since she was going directly to Raymond, who was waiting near Cherbourg, that I go on to London and probably stay there to study.

Before parting, however, we came to a tentative understanding that when I returned to France we would make a tour of Germany together. When the ship reached Southampton I went ashore and she journeyed on to Cherbourg.

Back in London, back to the same things I had so wanted to get away from forever. Back in Europe with no job and no money in sight except from Nancy. I knew I wanted to do the right thing but somehow I always missed by a thin margin. I knew some word, some decision, some move was lacking but I could not find it.

I only stayed in London about two weeks but while there I contacted John Payne, a Negro singer, and made arrangements to take singing lessons from a teacher he knew. But the lessons never took place. I changed my mind and informed Nancy that I was returning to France.

She was much taken up with Raymond but consented to my coming and made arrangements for our visit to Germany in the motorcar.

Despite a little trouble at the German frontier because I had forgotten to get a visa, the trip began very pleasantly indeed. I enjoyed the scenery and the people were so nice that

I formed the opinion Germans were the most excellent of all white people in so far as Negroes were concerned.

We moved in slow stages, stopping in many towns and villages. It was amusing to me for the inhabitants seemed to have never seen a black man driving a car before. Everywhere we stopped I created a sensation. Crowds immediately gathered and we were the center of interest.

We went to Munich and there saw Brian Howard, our old friend of the Austrian days, and the Honorable Eddy Gaythorne Hardy. Like Brian, Hardy is a nice boy. In Munich we went to many night clubs. Some of them were very interesting but not from an educational point of view. A great many of them were for men only. Instead of women waiting on and catering to men, there were only young boys.

This did not do for me but Eddy and Brian found companions and took them to the hotel. On one Saturday night when the regular weekend dance was in progress, Nancy and I went into the ballroom to see what it was all about. The place was crowded with couples in evening dress.

A little later Eddy came into the room dressed in a sweater and a pair of flannels. To my astonishment he asked a lady to dance with him. To my further astonishment she consented. He also told me an amazing story about the boy he had brought home from the café with him. It was so sordid that it won't bear repeating here. Nancy and I contented ourselves with sitting through the dance and watching the others, including the antics of Eddy.

The next day Eddy and Brian went away to the mountains but before leaving insisted that Nancy and I visit them later. We remained in the city for a few days and finally decided to motor up to see Brian and Eddy.

I found the trip very trying. The village where they were staying was very small and high up in the mountains. On our first night there a rather extraordinary incident took place.

It was after dinner and I was playing the piano in the

dining-room and singing softly. One by one the other guests retired for the night but not us.

I remained there playing when Eddy suddenly announced his intention of undressing and doing a dance. Without further words he proceeded to do so and then did a naked dance. I was flabbergasted. Nancy, however, seemed to take it all as a matter of course. Fortunately for all of us there were no other guests present.

Brian sensed my disapproval. He mentioned that I did not approve of their conduct. This was quite true and I took no pains in letting them know as much.

The following day Nancy and I motored back to Munich. We stayed there a day or so to further inspect the town and then started on to Berlin.

About half way there Nancy became so desirous of seeing her Raymond it appeared as though I would be left flat in Germany not only with the car but without any money.

Nancy came into the hotel where we were staying one afternoon and announced point blank:

"I am going back to Paris tonight."

Some sharp words followed and then just to show her obstinacy she telephoned the station and made reservations.

I admit that I was thoroughly disgusted with the woman at the time for she was demonstrating to the fullest one of her meanest traits—selfishness. I thought I was going to be stranded right there with a car, no money and speaking no German.

But the quarrel was patched up after a long altercation. I finally succeeded in bring her to reason. We continued our journey again together.

Berlin was an interesting place. We were only there for about four days but we saw a great deal of the city from what might be called a peculiar angle. From our hotel in the Unterden-Linden we journeyed to all parts of the town and visited every kind of place imaginable.

I recall one night particularly when we went out to

dance. At the place we went only men were allowed on one floor, only women were admitted on another. At another extraordinary place one part of it was reserved for women with women entertainers, another for women with men entertainers, and still another for men with men entertainers. It was very interesting if one could look at it all from a sane viewpoint.

I wanted to remain longer in Berlin but after the short stay we left for Hamburg. I wanted to linger and explore some of the interesting country around the city but Nancy wanted to return to Paris. So return to Paris we did.

Once back there I proposed to Nancy that I study music and French. She agreed and the tuition was paid in advance. But the program was never carried out because of numerous complications.

First of all Nancy had installed Raymond in a village near Chapelle-Réanville. She proposed to spend three or four days with Raymond and three or four days with me out of every week.

I could not see this and told her that I would never agree to any such arrangement. It was her idea that I stay in the country and motor to Paris for my lessons. I was to stay in the farm house and wait there until it pleased her to see me.

I thought the matter over and decided that it would never do so I told Nancy I was going to leave her and return to America.

We talked about it many hours and as Nancy was planning to visit America herself we arranged to meet early in the Spring in New York. She insisted that I take the auto.

We motored to Cherbourg and after a very pleasant last 24 hours together I embarked for America, taking the car with me. This was the third time I had made the journey in one year.

When we parted that time I think Nancy hated to see me leave her more than at any other time during all of our relations. I saw tears in her eyes as I waved good-bye from the deck. The parting affected me.

According to our plans when we met we were to take a trip to the West Indies together. Although I believed she was in earnest about this trip, I had absolutely no intention of going with her. I was through and I intended for my subsequent conduct to prove this parting would be the final one.

CHAPTER XIII

Hard Times in Washington

ONCE ON THE BOAT I vowed I had said good-bye to Nancy and Europe for the last time. For me the affair was finished. I could have stayed in France, yes, but as I saw it nothing could be gained by my doing so.

I was through, all through, and was going back to America to work and forget. As I thought it over I told myself that I had always been going somewhere to work and forget what had passed. I really meant to do it this time. I was going to Washington and begin again.

The voyage itself was quite pleasant. I was in great demand aboard ship as a pianist-entertainer by my fellow passengers and I always willingly played and sang when they asked.

Only one thing marred the trip. That was the idiotic and boorish behavior of the only other Negro passenger in the same class. He was one Rogers, reputedly an educated man, who claimed to be European correspondent for a number of Negro weekly papers in the United States. He sat at the same table as I in the dining room and made such a fool of himself that I almost left the table on several occasions, such was my disgust at his conduct.

A charming white woman with her lovely little baby boy of about six years sat at the table opposite us. This child for some unknown reason was attracted to me. He would leave his mother and come to me, climb upon my knee and prattle away at every meal. This embarrassed me to some extent for I did not know how the mother felt about this. I would cautiously caress the child's hair with my hands and quickly set him down again. The mother would only smile frankly and say nothing.

Rogers evidently did not like the exclusive attention the child paid me so he began spouting such phrases as:

"That's a wonderful boy! You can see he is going to be a great man by the shape of his head. He certainly does look intelligent, etc."

The mother sat silent with an expressionless face and I felt like kicking Rogers. He repeated this sort of thing so much that I dreaded the time to enter the dining room. I was on the verge of changing my table on several occasions but managed to stick it out. Rogers may have been a great journalist but in this instance he showed little tact and very poor judgment.

As the ship neared America I continually kept telling myself that I had said my final farewell to Europe and to Nancy. I had fully decided that I would take no trip to the West Indies with her and busied myself in mapping out my future activities in the United States.

I planned on going to Washington, throwing myself into the commercial musical business and start again where I had left off so many years ago. As I thought over my plans my enthusiasm grew. Long before the ship docked Europe and my adventures had become like a dream.

Landing in New York, I got my car through the customs without difficulty and after spending a hilarious night in Harlem, I hit the road for home—Washington.

All along the 175 miles of road I aroused great interest with my beautiful little French car. It still carried French license tags and caused a great deal of speculation among traffic police on the road and the towns through which I passed. They simply could not understand what it was all about.

On the outskirts of Philadelphia I passed a knot of highway policemen. They noticed the car, which was blue with red upholstering and with no running board. The top was back and every piece of metal was shining brightly.

One of the policemen decided to investigate so he followed me for about a mile on his motorcycle. Finally, he drew alongside and signaled for me to stop. He questioned me concerning my papers. I drew forth a great wallet of French identification papers, cards, permits, etc. Of these he could make nothing.

Finally, I produced a United States customs' receipt and a smile of understanding immediately appeared on his face.

"Where are you going, boy?"

I told him to Washington.

"Okay," he replied, "I know you are going to have a good time with the yaller gals down there." I smiled and drove on.

In Washington this car became an absolute nuisance to me. The police told me I need not change my tags and neither did I need an American driving permit. But being a black man and driving such a flashy car with French plates caused me to be constantly stopped and questioned by the police. They thought it was a French Embassy car and wondered what a black man was doing riding around Washington in it alone.

Everywhere I stopped people gathered and stared. As the days passed this sort of notoriety became unbearable so I put the car in a garage and left it there. Upon leaving for Europe the last time I gave it away.

I settled down in Washington and plunged into my work. I had seen my wife and as she seemed in the same frame of mind as on my first trip to America I thought it best to let things continue as they were. Besides, I was too busy to worry about something which had seemingly been settled before. I decided to let that "sleeping dog lie" as the saying goes.

I contacted musicians, joined the Musicians' Union, was elected to the board of directors and started practicing hard on the piano. I formed a partnership with a prominent Washington Negro musician and a starter. We had announcement cards printed and distributed among the wealthy and high social circles of Washington. Many of these persons I had known from the old days when I was in the entertainment business in the capital.

My days were full for I was busy getting things started. But after a month of activity I could see no results. I wondered at this. Not one of the aristocratic persons who had received our cards had given us an engagement. I finally discovered the cause.

My association with Nancy Cunard had received wide newspaper publicity in America, and many of the socially elite in Washington knew Lady Cunard personally. So upon finding that I was the self-same colored man who had figured in these reports they naturally would have none of me. I was told that some of them were offended at my temerity in even sending them a card offering my services. The proposition fell flat.

On the other hand the Negro people, who had received widely exaggerated versions of the affair, regarded me with mingled feelings. There was admiration from some, mostly men, contempt from others and lively interest from the younger feminine set.

Everyone knew about it. Fantastic tales had been told concerning my relations with Nancy while in Europe. Some of these made me laugh outright. The young colored women were curious to know what it was that had caused this supposed rich woman to care so much for me. My appearance in public always caused a murmur of whisperings.

"That's Henry Crowder. Who is he? Don't you know? He is the fellow that the rich white woman who owns the Cunard line is crazy about." Of course, all gross exaggerations. And from the men:

"Boy, you sho' is lucky," etc. . . . . If they had only known.

About this time in the spring of 1932 when things were beginning to get particularly boresome I received a letter from Nancy mailed in London stating she was prepared to come to New York and proceed to the West Indies as we had often talked about doing.

Having gone through all the disappointments and criticisms there in Washington and feeling in no mood to have them accentuated by her arrival, I wrote Nancy and told her of all the adverse publicity that had been going on. I further advised her that a trip to the United States at that time would do nothing but harm.

Her reply was one of the shapest reprimands I have ever received from her. She told me that she did not need my advice about coming to America; that she would do as she liked about the matter. She insisted on calling me a traitor and a rotter and said as far as she was concerned I could go to blazes. My reply to that was in few words. I wrote:

"My, what a temper you must have been in when you wrote that letter," and signed my name.

But warnings or no warnings, she sailed in company with John Banting, a London painter, and another nice boy. A few days later the trio arrived in New York. I wonder if she could have forseen all that would result from that trip of hers if she would have taken my advice and remained in Europe? It would take a prophet to tell.

I was in Washington and ignorant of the actual time of her arrival in America. I was soon enlightened, however, for newspaper articles of her activities in Harlem began to appear. Photographs of her were seen everywhere. Every sort of thing was printed.

She was hounded by reporters. They wanted a story. They wanted to know the name of her supposed Negro lover. They had heard he was a musician but they did not know who. They connected her with Paul Robeson but that story would not hold. A search was made everywhere. This Negro lover of the daughter of Lady Cunard, who was American born, must be found.

They worried the life out of poor Nancy. So much was she questioned that she told them her lover should be known just as John Doe. This of course did not satisfy so the hue and cry continued. Throughout all of this terrific newspaper notoriety I am sure Nancy managed to enjoy herself. Although she was hounded out of her hotel and shadowed through the streets, and in spite of the threatening and obscene letters which she received and the amazing articles printed about her, it is safe to say that she managed to have a good time just the same.

For a time all of this storm in New York blew over my head. I was glad for I did not want to become involved in the affair again. I had experienced all of the unpleasant scenes I cared to see on my first trip to America with Nancy. I remained as quietly as possible in Washington and said nothing.

But the news chasers finally found me. A very dapper young white man presented himself at my door one evening and asked for me. I told him who I was. He began asking questions about Nancy—if I knew her, when and where and what were our relations?

My replies were so non-committal that he confessed to me who he was and what he had come for. He showed me a telegram from a large New York newspaper instructing him to find Henry Crowder and get a story of his relations with Nancy Cunard.

I told him that I had known her in France in a very impersonal way; that I had not seen her for a long time and did not expect to see her any time soon. He thanked me and went away.

Then the same Negro Rogers with whom I had travelled across the ocean popped up at the house one evening. In a very crude manner he tried to inveigle me into giving him my photograph. I was sure he wanted it for some newspaper. His effort was wasted. I was not the easy mark he thought I was and my opinion of him as a clever man did not improve.

From the midst of all this excitement Nancy sent for me to come to New York and see her. She sent my fare one way but just enough money to buy the ticket. I spent the money and remained in Washington. After a short interval she again asked me to visit her in New York, again sending just the one way fare. I again spent the money and remained in Washington.

She then telegraphed that she was coming to Washington to see me. As I did not receive the telegram until after her scheduled arrival her trip down from New York was in vain. I then received a second telegram announcing that she was coming to Washington again. I was perfectly willing to see her but I got mixed-up in the time and place of her arrival so this second trip also failed to bring us together. She was extremely hurt over this and severely upbraided me about it afterwards.

My reason for not going to New York was that I did not wish to get involved in all of the scandal that was making the rounds about Nancy in the big city. As it was I was getting my share of the unpleasant notoriety in Washington.

Then came the sudden newspaper announcement that Nancy had left New York for Cuba with a Negro companion who was acting as bodyguard. It seems that he had to stage a fist-fight or almost one to keep the reporters from her cabin before the boat sailed.

She told me of this trip later in Europe. The newspapers claimed the Negro left a wife and one or two children behind in New England. I heard Nancy's version but could not understand it. In any case this man journeyed to the West Indies with her. In Jamaica she met Marcus Garvey, so she said, but stated she was not much impressed. After a brief stay in the West Indies, Nancy returned to New York *alone* and quickly slipped back to Europe.

During this whirlwind trip to America Nancy added three or four more Negroes to her list of potential lovers or admirers. These she told me because I was not on the scene. I am sure she also collected a great deal of material for her forthcoming Negro anthology.

For a period of seven or eight months after Nancy's return to Europe I received no word from her. In the meantime I had fallen into bad health and the financial crisis was at its worst. I was among the unemployed. My morale got lower and lower. I was very despondent. My nerves went to pieces. I lost energy and ambition. I even reached the stage where moonshine whiskey was more important to me than food. I did not care whether I lived or died. I lost my appetite and could not eat. I was gradually dying on my feet. I had forgotten Nancy.

Then one day my reason failed and, unconscious, they took me to a hospital. I was revived and taken home but a few minutes after reaching there, I again collapsed. The ambulance was called again. The doctor again revived me and advised that I be sent to a mental hospital for observation. My friends refused to let this happen.

I drank a large glass of moonshine and again felt normal. However, I was still far from well and my stomach refused to take solid food. I had no money and no ambition to make any. Besides, I was not physically able to do any work.

Down, down, down the ladder of respectability I was sliding. I lingered in the old haunts I had known years before in the red-light district. But I was lower then than before. I would have gladly played in a whorehouse had there been any.

I touched what must have been bottom for me for I finally decided to try bootlegging. But I could not stick with it. There must have still been a spark of respectability left for I simply could not tolerate the low class of people with whom I had to associate. After an abortive attempt I gave it up.

Aimlessly drifting, a drink here and a bite to eat there; gaunt, greedy poverty staring me in the face every moment; I knew not what to do nor where to turn. I really did want to die.

Then out of a clear sky came a cable from somewhere in the South of France from Nancy.

"Where are you?" it said. "Very worried must have news."

As an answer was prepaid I replied. Correspondence followed and Nancy assisted me financially after I made known my condition. Some fairly regular letters between us followed. In one of these she mentioned the possibility of my returning to Europe.

But despite the conditions under which I was living I told her I would return on one condition only—that I had something to do from which I could derive an independent income. I had seen too much of life with her before to want to go back and live under those circumstances again.

In ensuing correspondence Nancy proposed that I take charge of a bureau in London for Negroes that would be sort of a welfare center. Included was to be a book shop, information bureau, a register of hotels and boarding houses where Negroes coming to London might stay, reading room, etc. This was to be worked in connection with the Negro Welfare League of London but I was to be in charge.

With that definite promise I thought it better for me to return. All arrangements were completed as regards salary, etc., and I accepted. I considered it as a God-send to me in my then sorry condition so with my steamship fare prepaid I once again left New York for Europe.

CHAPTER XIV

Back to Nancy

WHAT A DIFFERENCE. When I sailed out of New York the first time the future seemed filled with innumerable good things. When I sailed out that time it appeared as time to come, as life to serve, as a means to the inevitable end.

No, there was no hilarity in my being then; there was no shouting or laughing companions; there was only a faint hope that life might serve me better where I was going than in the place I had left behind.

Back to Nancy; back to the old quarrels that I knew were bound to come; back to a life with exciting times but also back to a life that I could not help but believe would hold its disappointments and false illusions.

When I landed at Cherbourg I went straight to Paris. After spending two days there I journeyed to London where I was met at Victoria station by Nancy. I had not seen her for nearly 20 months.

Nancy, the woman I had once tried to kiss and had been kissed for my trouble. She looked older, she looked more tired, but she was the same.

No sooner had I greeted her than she quickly informed me that a party was being held that night in celebration of my arrival and as it was rather late we must rush. Nancy, always rushing; always doing something. My bags were dropped at her apartment in the West Central district and we proceeded to the party.

I was sorry later that I had gone to that party. It opened up an entirely new phase of Nancy's curious life to me. The atmosphere, the people, the language: they were all new and strange to me and I immediately found them displeasing. Still, there I was so there was nothing to do but make the best of it.

The party, which was given at the house of one of Nancy's black African friends by the name of Douglass Papafio, proved to be rather a drunken affair. There were other African and West Indian Negroes present but aside from Papafio's wife the other women were white.

I was mildly surprised to find that Nancy was now associating with African Negroes for before that, as far as I know, her colored acquaintances had all been Americans. I don't know why I should have been even mildly surprised after my former experiences with Nancy but I remember that I was.

Everyone there had been looking forward to seeing me. Whether I lived up to their expectations about me I don't know. But I do know that despite the depths to which I had sunk in America, despite the slips I had made down the ladder I was trying to climb, something in me would not let me like the people I met that night. Even though I was there because a white woman had been kind to me when I needed help I could not help feeling that I was superior to many who attended that party.

When the evening ended we returned to a large studio flat in which Nancy lived in the West Central district. When we arrived, Nancy, to my surprise, informed me that she was leaving that same morning for the Continent.

It was Raymond again. She intimated that their relations were strained and that she was going over to try and straighten matters out. It seemed that Raymond's father had died and left some property which fell to Raymond. He had sold the property and, having a feeling of independence, had found himself a girl friend nearer to his age and undoubtedly more to his liking. He had evidently decided it was time his affair with Nancy ended. She went away to see him, undoubtedly sensing the end of their romance.

Her premonition proved to be true. When she returned she told me she was through with Raymond; that he had become a snob and many other things I would not like anyone to call me. As on many other occasions, I felt sorry for Nancy then. Her love affair with Raymond had lasted for a long time and he had deserted her.

Before she left for the Continent she showed me a small bundle of clothes and told me if anyone called and asked for them to say she was away and deliver them to the person calling. During the day of her departure I answered the doorbell and was confronted by a bespectacled young white man of rather pleasant appearance who asked for Nancy.

I told him she was away and inquired if he had come for a bundle of clothing. He admitted shyly that the bundle was his but was hesitant about taking it. I told him it was alright for him to take the clothes as Nancy had instructed me to give them to him.

But he still hesitated and did not seem to know just what to do. Finally he said he would await her return before taking them and went away.

This young man, I later learned, was Edgell Rickword, a young English Communist writer who was at that time one of Nancy's lovers. It appeared that he had been living at the studio but upon my arrival was compelled to at least temporarily vacate.

This amused me very much. I could not help thinking "just another one of the boys." I certainly had nothing against the lad but his naivete amused me because I knew he had not yet learned all there was to know about Nancy.

When I knew the boy later he proved to be a very fine chap. He was a good writer and a great consumer of booze. I saw much of him while I was in London and we became very good friends.

The impression I gained of Nancy's new Negro friends at the first party proved to be right for as I came to know them better I knew I could never get along with them. They were all a very nondescript lot. I was mildly surprised that

Nancy was associating with such persons and especially in her home town.

But she took great interest in them. She was instrumental in gathering 15 or 20 of these Negroes together at her flat who were to organize themselves into a Committee to be in some way affiliated with the Communist party. Chris Jones, a big black West Indian Negro, who had drifted to England via the United States, was chosen as chairman of the committee.

Chris, who had been a sailor, could tell many amusing stories of his life in New York and of the times when he was an assistant in the gambling dens of that city. He was a Communist and had ambitions to become an orator. He had spoken quite extensively in England in the interest of Communism, I believe. He was not an illiterate man but very stupid.

At least I thought so, but Nancy considered him very brilliant. She once told me she thought he should be subsidized, meaning I suppose, that someone should support him so he could confine his activities to speaking. I thought him a poor speaker and knew he was an uneducated and untrained one. At every possible opportunity Nancy was seeing this man.

The committee meetings continued but I absented myself from them. I wanted nothing to do with that sort of thing. Very soon, in her usual fashion, Nancy became disgusted with the whole business and dropped it forthwith.

And with her loss of interest in that project all of the plans that had brought me back to Europe went by the board with scarcely any comment being made. Nancy declared to me that henceforth she was putting all of her interests in her book—the anthology.

So there I was again—right back in the same position I had sworn I would never find myself in again. Stranded, in a foreign country where I could not get a working permit even if I found a job. The future looked about as bright as the moon in eclipse. What was I to do? I stuck.

These events covered a period of about three months and during that time Nancy realized that I did not wish to associate with her Negro friends. Her resentment of my attitude began to make itself felt.

She proposed taking a flat with Rickword. I offered no word in opposition to the idea but flatly refused to live in the same building with them myself. But that did not stop Nancy. The flat was secured but before moving in with Rickword she went away to the country to work on the anthology.

Bad or good luck, while away she made me the generous allowance of five shillings (about $1.25) a day to live on. This of course did not include the room rent. But out of the five shillings I was to eat two meals, buy smokes, pay car fare, laundry, go to the movies and buy a drink now and then.

"Hell," I thought, "five shillings a day and no way of bettering myself." I could not save enough of that to leave nor could I work at my profession because I had no permit. Many were the nights during those times that I wished I had remained in America and rotted rather than be in such circumstances.

While she was away in the country she had various people down from London to visit her. These included her boy friend Rickword, Papafio, the African Negro—with whom she seemed to be infatuated—and various other people. She invited me to visit her but I refused to go.

Simultaneously with Nancy's leasing the flat for herself and Rickword I secured separate quarters for myself. I found a very nice place in Regents Park near the residence of John Payne, the colored American singer. Nancy visited this place of mine on only two occasions during the entire five or six months I lived there.

When she came back from the country she became very busy getting the flat ready for occupancy. The place selected was literally a series of loft rooms in Percy Street. The floors were of coarse boards and sagged in crazy fashion while the ceiling was very low. Two bedrooms, a large sitting room, a large kitchen and a bathroom made up the ensemble.

The furniture, rugs, books, paintings, hangings, African art objects, in fact, practically everything was ordered moved from her country house in France to England. After tremendous difficulties which included taking out a door and sawing a couch bed in two, the stuff was finally placed in the rooms.

Floors were painted, new book shelves constructed, rugs cleaned and stored. Besides the great expense, this all entailed a tremendous amount of work. I bore the brunt of all this work. But it was all finished and she moved in with Rickword.

Nancy then graciously consented to give me in addition to the five shillings a day another pound a week (about $5) to cover my separate room rent. The conditions under which I had consented to return to Europe had long since been forgotten and true to form Nancy began grumbling about what she was giving me.

She wanted me to be one of her lovers in the intimate sense of the word and I absolutely refused. Not only was I afraid but I certainly had no intention of doing anything like that as long as there were so, so many other men in her life.

Too, I would not consent to take part in the Communist demonstrations which she and her cohorts were supporting. I refused to parade with them or go to protest meetings. I only nominally supported her efforts to aid the Negro boys involved in the Scottsboro case. I found some excuse whenever possible to prevent my going any place with her at all.

Although she was keeping me I felt I owed Nancy nothing as she had certainly not kept her promises. I wanted so badly to be completely finished with the entire affair but could do nothing but bide my time at that stage.

In any case, she and Rickword seemed to be getting along charmingly and I had met a lovely English colored girl who was absorbing every minute of my time. Nancy knew of my affair with this colored girl but made no comment aside from the fact that she thought her very nice and that I seemed to be very fond of her. Nancy was right.

Nancy's life in London during this period was one terrific rush. She was up to her ears in work on the anthology. She fussed and fumed; cursed and damned. The book, according to her, should be ready before Christmas—it was finally finished the first part of the following year, 1934.

In this work Rickword did yeoman service. He helped her immensely. He was very kind and obliging. I often looked at him working away with sincere pity. I knew from experience that regardless of how hard he worked that his time to be "dumped" would come eventually. Whether he realized this I had no way of knowing but I did feel sorry for him for I felt he was being played for a dupe.

Christmas came. As I had so regularly found some excuse for not going out with Nancy she informed me well in advance of a Christmas dinner party to be given at Papafio's house. I promised her I would go but was fully determined in my own mind not to associate with THAT crowd any more than I could help. She was persistent in her efforts to have me mix with her colored friends in London and I was equally as persistent in not doing so.

The night of the party arrived. I was home alone. I put out all the lights, locked all the rooms of my flat with the exception of the bedroom door and went to bed. I did not lock the bedroom door as it opened on the hall and I thought no one but my colored girl friend would think of coming through it uninvited.

I was wrong. Nancy arrived and asked the landlady for me. She was told that I was probably out. But to see for herself Nancy came up the stairs and finding the bedroom door unlocked opened it and came in. She switched on the light. I played at sleeping but to no avail. After a short discussion I climbed out of bed, dressed, and went to the party.

If there ever was a time I wanted to be free to do as I wished it was that night. I could not help feeling like a "hunted man." I wanted freedom; I wanted to get away . . . but I couldn't.

We were late. But Nancy was always late to everything so it did not matter. The party lasted until daybreak. I escorted

Nancy home. Rickword was away for the holidays but he might just as well have been there on the spot for all that it meant to me. I know that Nancy must have had some queer feelings about my conduct but my mind was made up on the matter of intimacy.

When the book was finally finished there came a lull in Nancy's activities and I knew that trouble could be expected from some angle. For some weeks she had been hinting to me that she did not see how she could continue giving me the two pounds fifteen shillings each week.

She also started criticizing Rickword. He had suddenly developed all sorts of faults. I knew the end was in sight for him. She was rummaging in her mind for something to do. London was too dull for her. She was tired of the flat. She was flitting here and there to every gathering that even smelled of Communism.

As time passed she became more and more restive. The great hunger march of the year was in progress and daily getting closer to London. One afternoon I visited her flat and was amazed to see her dressed in a most outlandish costume. It was a mixture of everything. A man's overcoat, an aviator's helmet, overshoes, a woman's dress, mufflers, scarfs and gloves. Really astonished, I asked what was up.

Very mysteriously she told me she was off to join the hunger marchers and intended "doing a few miles" with them. I was to tell no one. The conglomeration of clothing, she told me, was not only for a disguise but also for warmth. Off she went with a small movie camera in her hand. "Well, Well," said I to myself. "What the dickens will she do next?"

After a lapse of two or three days she returned. When I learned that she was back I went to the flat to see her. She was in her room and Rickword was conversing with her from his room across the hall. I was standing there talking to her when I heard a key placed in the entrance door. I wondered who on earth had a key besides Nancy and Rickword.

Soon there was a heavy masculine tread mounting the stairs. I very interestedly awaited the outcome of this extraordinary happening. Presently a roughly dressed young man entered. Placing some money on the table, he explained that he could not get the things he had been sent for so "there was the change." He was perfectly at ease and Nancy introduced us. I could never remember his name, however, so I always called him "Hunger Marcher" when reference was made to him.

In spite of the fact that I should have been accustomed to Nancy's lightning change of lovers, I never ceased to marvel at them. She had gone on the hunger march, grabbed one of the marchers and brought him home with her. All of this despite the fact that Rickword was still living in the flat and was still her lover.

However, Rickword apparently took the matter in good grace. He and I left the flat shortly afterwards to get a drink. I asked him if the young man was a new lover of Nancy's. I don't remember if he answered the question or not but he seemed hurt. He later told me he was very much in love with Nancy.

He made a quick recovery though. Hardly had "Hunger Marcher" moved in than Rickword found himself a girl and installed her in his room in the flat. Good work for Rickword but not so good for Nancy.

Just as I expected, a day or two of this foursome and Nancy and Rickword's girl had serious differences. Soon afterwards Rickword arrived home one day to find himself and girl friend literally "thrown out." Nancy could give it but she could not take it. The flat was in Nancy's name so Rickword and Company had to go. After that events began to move faster.

On one occasion Nancy and her cousin, Victor, became embroiled in an argument at an inter-racial dance where I was the master of ceremonies. Two colored women were involved and a particularly nasty scene resulted. Some unprintable epithets were hurled about and the dances, which were run weekly, were suspended.

Nancy, as a rule, brought "Hunger Marcher" to these

dances and at one of the first ones gave him a foretaste of
what she had in store for him by leaving the dance without
him. She later told me she had a rendezvous with a taxi-driver
(white) who was an ex-policeman. She said he was a good
man.

I met him later and found him to be even better than
she had pictured him. He had an invalid wife whom he
adored. I often saw him at night driving his cab in London
and always inquired about the condition of his wife. Although
he had no hopes of her recovering, he took great pleasure in
making life as pleasant as possible for her. In this instance,
love and loyalty prevailed over sordid selfishness.

Although the advent of "Hunger Marcher" meant nothing to me the feeling between Nancy and myself became
more aggravated. She repeatedly told me that I did not care
for her which was true. Furthermore, I took no pains to hide
it. She tried every device she was selfishly capable of trying
to cause me to change. But it was no use. I held aloof. The
parade of lovers that I had witnessed had long since killed
even any pretense of feeling I may have had for her.

As I foresaw, she finally gave up and suddenly informed
me that she was leaving for France the next day and that I
need not expect any further assistance from her. Without
further ado, she said good-bye, and taking "Hunger Marcher"
with her, set out for the Continent.

But I was one jump ahead that time. I knew all of this
was coming so I had quietly laid plans to take care of myself
when the break eventually came. The work I could do was
not much but I did manage to keep from going hungry. So
I quickly adjusted myself to the changed conditions and continued on my even way.

A few weeks later she wrote me that she had interceded
with Maurice, the owner of the Boeuf-sur-le-Toit in Paris,
and that he had agreed to engage me if I would come to Paris.
Subsequently my railroad fare arrived. But again just railroad
fare. As I had done before in America I kept the money and
remained in England.

For the next seven or eight months I did not know where she was—whether she was dead or alive. I managed to eke out a living in London, waiting for the day when something better would turn up. I thought I had seen the last of her when, in her characteristic way, I suddenly received a letter asking what I was doing. I answered and contact was again established.

A later letter asked me if I would go travelling with her—to Russia or Haiti? I replied that travelling did not interest me; that I had returned to Europe to make money and that the idea still persisted.

By that time I had gotten around the permit question and had secured a fairly decent job in a theatre orchestra. I certainly had no intention of leaving that to go running around the country with her. No word was received from her after that for some time so I kept quietly to my own business.

In late summer of 1934 she wrote again, asking if I would visit her for a few days in Boulogne as she was very ill and wanted to see me. My fare arrived and I crossed the Channel for regardless of all the ups and downs we had gone through I could not turn down her request if she was ill. We spent the week-end together.

I found her very ill indeed and advised her to go to London for treatment. This she agreed to do and arrived in London a very sick woman. When she saw a competent doctor he immediately ordered her to a nursing home with complete rest. She remained in a precarious state for some weeks.

I felt sorry for her then. I hate to see anyone suffer and despite the aches and discomforts she had caused in my life I would have done most anything she might have asked then if I would have helped.

During these weeks the question of travelling was discussed again. I reiterated the necessity of my doing something to earn money and that I could not afford to waste further time running around the world.

She hinted at settling a small sum of money on me. I

told her that would certainly make me face the future with more assurance. But the matter ended there.

However, this suggestion to settle a small sum on me caused me to consider her plan to travel in a different light. With that in the back of my head I decided to return to France with her when she was able to travel.

From the nursing home we were driven to Eastbourne on the sea where we stayed two weeks. We then returned to London, put all of the furniture in storage, closed the flat and crossed into France again.

CHAPTER XV

A Peculiar Woman

I F I HAD NEEDED anything to further illustrate the almost unbelievable decisions the extraordinary mind of this most uncommon woman could make, the few months I spent in London had surely supplied them.

She had discarded the original idea that had brought me to England as easily as a person would throw off a winter coat when summer arrives. Although she did render me assistance of a sort while I was there the obligation she assumed in bringing me to London sat very lightly on her shoulders. She had brought me there but because I was of no use to her she left me to shift for myself.

For my part, I should have known and realized what would follow when I left Washington and placed myself in her hands. Had I allowed it, I would have again become clay in her hands to mould me into the shape she wished. I have my stars to thank that I did not. Otherwise, even to this day, I suppose, perhaps I would still be in Nancy's "entourage" instead of sitting and writing these words.

It is not difficult to recall incidents which happened during those months which amply illustrate how extremely absorbed she was in her own life and how unusual many of her decisions.

Evelyn Strachey, a former Labor member of the British parliament, lived near the House of Commons. He had just married an American woman by the name of Esther Murphy—since divorced and remarried. Soon after her arrival in London with Evelyn she achieved a reputation as a talker. She had strong political leanings and was not a bit reticent about letting everyone who met her know her views. She usually insisted on talking politics until everyone within hearing was more than bored. She was also quite an historian. Among other accomplishments, she had the tactical maneuvers of the Battle of Waterloo at her fingertips.

I met her after her marriage to Strachey. I had met him on a previous occasion I think and once had the privilege of being shown around the House of Commons by him in company with Nancy. Nancy and Strachey were, and I think still are, great friends.

Mr. and Mrs. Strachey invited us to their home one evening. I can't recall whether for dinner or just for music and drinks. The evening was moving alone pleasantly enough when Nancy and Strachey wandered out of the room, leaving Esther and me alone. At first no notice was taken of their absence. But after a lapse of almost an hour we naturally became uncomfortable and then downright uneasy.

I did not know what to do or say. Esther maintained an outward urbanity but I could easily imagine that all was not serene in her mind. Finally, after what seemed ages, they returned. The explanation of the long absence was that they had entered a room downstairs and a servant had unknowingly locked them in and went away. They stated that they were unable to get out or attract attention. Finally, according to their story, they climbed out the window and entered the house again by the front door.

The story passed for the evening but the next day I brought the matter up when Nancy and I were alone. I told her I thought her action in leaving her hostess for so long was selfishness in the extreme and furthermore that it was highly suspicious. She flew into a terrible rage.

"Do you mean to insinuate that anything improper took place?" she stormed at me.

I replied that I was not insinuating anything but that her hostess seemed to spend some uncomfortable moments during her long absence from the music room.

In her anger Nancy grabbed the telephone, called the

Stracheys, and told them what I had said. And because of that she cancelled a proposed joint trip to the south of France that was being planned. I was glad the trip was called off for that one evening had already given me too many unpleasant moments.

Another instance of the unusual things Nancy did while I was in London the last time was illustrated by her associations with a certain type of Negroes. I could not stand her Negro friends and this displeased her very much. Particularly, I did not like one Joe Pollard in whom she was interested. He had a bad police record and shortly after I arrived in London she escorted me to a low dive which was managed by Pollard. I immediately saw the character of the place and refused to take off my hat while there, insisting that we leave immediately.

This same Pollard got into trouble with the police soon afterwards for fighting and was sentenced to three months imprisonment. Nancy was very much affected by this. She argued with me stoutly in his defense when I told her that the colored people I knew informed me that Pollard had received only what was coming to him.

Then one morning about three o'clock she entered the studio and awakened me. I noticed she was looking particularly depressed and asked:

"What is the matter?"

She did not reply but presently I saw tears coming into her eyes. I could not imagine what had gone wrong and insisted on an explanation. I finally secured the following story between sobs:

She had gone to visit Pollard in jail. It seemed that all she could get out of him was incoherent demands that she get him out of the place. She was crying because she was unable to induce the authorities to accept a fine for his release and felt miserable because of his incarceration. I blandly told her that he was probably where he ought to be.

Later, she actually approached a lawyer on the subject of appealing the sentence imposed on Pollard who was al-

legedly one of the most notorious Negro characters in London. The lawyer advised her to save her money.

I have since been told by many colored people in London that Nancy had been on rather intimate terms with Pollard and she herself told me that there was something about him that she liked very much.

Judging from the class of Negroes to whom she introduced me I could not help assuming that something in those low types attracted her. Whether it was because of her desire to help them that she associated with them I shall never know.

Conversely, she would never tolerate the high class, highly educated Negroes as her associates for long. But high or low, white or black, when it was a matter of her feelings nothing was allowed to interfere.

She told me once of meeting a Negro dancer by the name of Chic Horsey (now dead) on the Riviera at the time she was with Raymond. She said he attracted her tremendously. He wanted her to go away with him and she told me she almost did so. Later, she voiced her regret for not having done so, saying:

"A person should always do what they want to, regardless of anyone else." This was one of her pet theories and I really believed she tried to live up to it as much as possible.

She further told me that the kind of man she wanted was one who would agree that she was in the right regardless of what she did. I told her she would have one made to order if she ever expected to find a man like that.

Such a peculiar woman with more than peculiar ideas. I have seen her become intensely interested and enthusiastic about a person's appearance and then go to any amount of bother to meet them. Subsequently there would be meetings for drinks, dinners and chats. She would be high in her praise of that person in the beginning. Then just as quickly she would say her interest in that person was dead.

After I became acquainted with this trait when she would ask me what I thought of someone I would always reply, "opinion reserved." I knew she would surely change her ideas sooner or later.

As for me, she always said I was her "tree." She stated that after she had gone afield and had become tired and weary of a new attraction she always wanted to know that she could return to the security of her "tree."

That was supposed to be my role in her life. What a difficult one to play. It was distasteful to me in its entirety and one I certainly never fully accepted.

I remember one time in Paris it became the vogue to go to a small cabaret in the Montmartre called the Music Box. Nancy became a regular client of the place and always took her friends there. On several occasions I noticed that as soon as her party was seated she would disappear down the stairs and stay an interminably long time. She left the members of her party to amuse themselves as best as they could.

One night at this place she disappeared as usual. She remained away so long that people in the party began to wonder where she was. I decided to investigate. On descending the stairs I discovered her in very earnest conversation with Fred, the Negro cook.

She had entirely forgotten her party upstairs and everyone there who had come to the café in answer to her invitation. I remonstrated with her and she very angrily rejoined the party. This determination to please herself seemed to be one of the driving motives of Nancy's life.

When we left England for Paris no definite plans had been made. We stayed two or three days in a cheap, dingy hotel in Montmartre and then went on to Chapelle-Réanville. The place was in shambles. The grounds were overgrown with weeds, the well was nearly dry and all the drains around the house were clogged with dirt and leaves. The outside of the house presented a sad sight.

I had not seen the place for over three years. On the inside, the place was in an awful state. There were cobwebs everywhere. Even dirty dishes and cooking utensils she had used during her occupancy the previous spring and summer had been left unwashed. (She was then with John Banting and George Padmore, the Negro journalist and member of the Communist Party.)

We made shift for a day or two, returned to Paris, spent one day and then caught a train for Cannes. We spent several days there searching for a cheap place to live and finally settled in Mougins a few miles up in the mountains north of Cannes.

From a geographical point, Mougins is a very picturesque place but the hotel in which we lived was as uncomfortable as could be imagined. We went to the Riviera expecting sunshine and warmth. Instead we found cold, rain and even snow.

Nancy was suffering from the effects of a treatment she was receiving from a doctor in Cannes. The rooms were unheated save for a small wood fire and were bleak and quite cheerless.

In my room the only place to keep warm was in bed so when I was up I spent most of my time in the bistro drinking the strong liquor of the country—vin du pays. Each morning I would take a strong drink in hot water to enable me to brave the chill of the room.

Nancy spent a great deal of the time out of doors walking up and down the mountains on which we lived. I accompanied her on the walks occasionally but generally I remained indoors, either practicing the piano or playing billiards with the natives in the bistro. I did manage to compose the words and music for a new song.

The question of money was a daily one. Nancy was continually speaking of the smallness of her income. In fact, one of the reasons for going to Cannes was to try to get a job for me in the Boeuf cabaret that was owned by Maurice of Paris. We discovered, however, that he had sold the place so that possibility ended.

We then went to Nice to contact agents. At the same

time I wrote to several professional friends but obtained no results. I then took a quick trip back to Paris to give an audition for a job in Lille but was prevented from taking the position for the lack of a working permit.

The trip cost some seven or eight hundred francs and as it failed to produce results it caused additional acrimonious words between us. Upon my return to Cannes I informed Nancy that in order for me to be in a position to get work it was necessary for me to be in Paris.

I finally convinced her of this and after a few more days we again journeyed north through flurries of snow. The trip back was broken at Marseilles where we spent a large part of the night in the underworld quarter.

In Paris we settled in a small hotel apartment having two bedrooms and a bath. Nancy was very fond of the place but I disliked it very much. It reminded me too greatly of many other places where I had lived under the same circumstances.

It again reminded me that I had once more given up a job which supported me to travel with Nancy. It made me recall the small settlement she had once said she would make on me but never did. It reminded me of everything I had tried to run away from and there I was in exactly the same position again.

The inevitable question of plans for the future again came up for consideration. Again and again she told me of her lack of money. She said she did not know what she was going to do. But regardless of her stated financial difficulties she still took people to dinner.

Things came to such a pass that I requested she give me 25 francs a day and I would buy my own meals as she always quarrelled if the bill for two meals came to as much as 20 francs. She consented to this but even then on many occasions I received the 25 francs in installments.

In an effort to help her I proposed that I get a small apartment for myself as she had decided to return to Chapelle-Réanville and live there. I told her it would be impossible for me to live in the country as I must be in Paris in order to get work. I promised, however, to help her get the place in order for occupancy.

Accordingly, I found me a small place and then went to the country with her to help clean the house. I remained three or four days and did some of the hardest work of my life. I swept and scrubbed floors, washed dishes and windows, painted woodwork, cleaned walls, painted stoves and cleaned the lawn. At the end of the four days I journeyed back to Paris, leaving her alone in the house.

In a day or two she came to Paris and declared that it was impossible for her to stay in the country alone. We set about immediately to solve the problem as it was impossible for me to stay down there with her.

Anna, Nancy's old maid, was written to and while awaiting the answer Nancy thought of asking Fred, the former cook at the Music Box, to come to the country with her as cook and man of all work.

She told him she could only pay him 10 francs a day with room and board. She thought this might work as Fred was out of a job and needed help. Fred was approached on the matter and everything seemed to be satisfactorily settled. In the meantime Fred was escorting Nancy to night clubs and to the theatre. She was having dinner with him and meeting him for cocktails. To all of this I had not the slightest objection for such things had now become part of the day's routine with me. The only thing Nancy could have done to surprise me was not to meet and run around with new men but to stop such practices.

Everything at the house in the country was then practically in order and it was ready for occupancy. Suddenly Nancy informed me that the deal with Fred was all off. Why? It seemed that Fred wanted some advance money to pay over-due room rent and probably to settle other bills. In fact, he became so insistent that Nancy became angry and called the whole thing off.

She vowed that she would have nothing further to do

with Fred but in consideration of the fact that she had tentatively engaged him she sent him a check for 300 francs and called it a day.

A French woman of the village was engaged to come for a few hours daily to do the cleaning and Nancy decided to do her own cooking. A young French couple, close friends of Nancy's, also went down to stay with her for a time. The girl was very ill and shortly after going there collapsed and had to be removed to the hospital. She had attempted a self-imposed cure for drugs I was told.

I was very naturally spending most of my time in Paris with Nancy coming up for week-ends. These fortnightly meetings grew increasingly unpleasant. She was continually groaning about something.

Why was I not working, she had no money, etc., were her chief complaints. It began to be a nightmare and I was fast losing my patience. I think I can take as much as the next man but these meetings were getting to be more than I could stand.

On one occasion I secured a contract to work for two days in Cambrai and told Nancy about it. Instead of showing any pleasure, it seemed to anger her. But I should have known that.

Many times before I had heard her yell about me going to work and as soon as I started she did what she could to stop me. This had happened years before when I was working at the Bateau Ivre. It was also Nancy who had enticed me away from a good job at the Plantation.

She was in Paris the night before I was to leave for Cambrai about five o'clock the next morning. In company with an African Negro we went to dinner. Afterwards we went to Montmartre for coffee and drinks. I got along famously with the young African and I am positive that Nancy did not relish the friendship that seemed to spring up between us two black men.

She left the table. While she was away this young man and I agreed on a tentative program for some future activities together from a racial standpoint. Upon her return we advised her of our plans but she was rather reserved in her comments.

The evening came to an end with my new African acquaintance going away and Nancy coming to my apartment. It was late so I packed my case and took up a book to read for the little time that remained before I would have to leave to catch my train.

Nancy was in the bathroom. She presently came into the bedroom where I was and without the slightest semblance of a reason said:

"We don't like each other any more so we might as well call it quits."

I was astonished. The evening had been pleasant and no one was drunk so I wondered what was wrong. I asked her to please not start quarrelling as I was in no mood for it. She continued in the same strain and finally announced that she was going away at that very moment.

It was raining very hard and the hour was then about 4:30 A.M. I tried to persuade her not to go by pointing out how late it was; that pretty soon I would be gone and she would have the place for herself. She was pacified for a moment and started to undress, mumbling all the while.

Suddenly she said something I could not stand and a sharp, vicious exchange of words followed. She grabbed what pieces of clothing she had discarded and quickly putting them on again, stated that she was leaving.

I told her to go to hell and stay there. And I meant every word of it.

Out she went.

I immediately fell asleep. Luckily for me she returned or I would have missed my train. When she entered I jumped up, snatched my bag, said good-bye and was off.

Returning from Cambrai I found a note on the table telling me that she was through. She had informed the concierge that she was not responsible for the flat and that any arrangements I made would be on my own.

She did, however, leave me a check for 200 francs and

stated that I would get one for the same amount every week until June 1, 1935. She stated she could do no more after that. This meant about six weekly checks of 200 francs each.

Her method of arriving at this figure was characteristic of her. In London she gave me five shillings a day for expenses including food. This amounted to one pound 15 shillings a week. Later when she took the flat with Rickword, she added another pound a week for my separate room rent. This was a total of two pounds 15 shillings a week—about $17.50.

When she exchanged that amount into francs it came to the magnificent sum of 200 francs. The question of exchange rates or the difference in the cost of living meant nothing to her.

Furthermore, and more characteristic of her, the following week the check did not arrive at all and I was left penniless. I gave up the flat and pawned some clothing in order to eat.

After Nancy had informed me she had transferred the last 200 francs to my name at the bank I went there to collect it. I was told that the transfer had been cancelled. I know nothing of her reason for doing this but it once more illustrated how quickly she could change her mind regardless of the consequences.

I have seen Nancy on two occasions since. I passed her in the street in Montmartre once and we spoke briefly. The last time I was with her we went to a dinner party together in the northern suburbs of Paris.

I left the party early, promising to see Nancy in her hotel later that night but I knew when I made the promise I would never go near her place again. When I asked her why she wanted me to come to her hotel she said very glibly:

"Well, you say you have no hotel to go to!"

"I know," I said, "but what difference does one night make; what about tomorrow?"

"I don't know," she answered, "I am going to London tomorrow morning!"

I said no more to her, but my thoughts as I wandered back to the subway and to Montmartre were never meant for these pages. I was again stranded but I did not care for something told me that parting was the final one. I never intended to see her again unless it happened to be by chance. I still hold to that decision.

I had no money with which to return home so there was nothing for me to do but remain in Paris and look for work. It was not long, however, before luck again looked my way. At least it appeared that way.

I had been rehearsing with a band that secured a contract to play in Rome for the summer. Once again I was headed for Italy. Again I hoped, as I had done many times before, that the job would prove to be a good one and would lead to something worthwhile. As I travelled south from Paris my spirits began to rise. Going to a new job; leaving all the past behind me; starting a new page that I resolved to fill with work and accomplishments.

The band opened in Rome. It only played two days. Whether the Abyssinian question had anything to do with it I don't know but I do know that our contracts were broken and I was without work.

Stranded again. And this time in a strange city. Had it not been for a friend in Paris whom I wired for money I might have still been there. Either that or dumped back over the French border into the country from which I had come.

While waiting in Rome for my return fare I had plenty of time to think over the past and particularly the last six years I had spent in Europe.

"What a mess I had made of my life," I thought. "How all of my hopes and ambitions had been shattered. . . ." I had staked everything on the whims of a white woman and had lost.

I realized that I was no younger and had made no progress in my profession. My talents had gone neglected and I was out of touch. I reviewed all of the incidents that had passed since I first came to Europe. I had to admit to myself that I was a failure.

But the trip back to Paris did me good. It helped me to

draw my belt up another notch and put myself in the right frame of mind to face the future.

I have a very staunch white man friend here in Paris who has promised to see me through and so far he has faithfully kept his word. He has kept the fire of hope alive and is ably assisted by my colored girl friend who has encouraged me tremendously all along.

I am now back in the run again. I secured one job in a restaurant but lost it because I had no working permit. But there are others and I am after them. In the meantime I have managed to get enough work playing in bars for private parties and dances to keep me going. I have just secured a temporary place singing and playing at Harry's New York Bar which I hope will prove to be permanent.

So I'm on my way. Let the future bring what it may, I'm ready to meet it.

white women ✓

In Retrospect

O NCE, IN MY INNOCENCE, I thought all women were good and honorable. They had a high and almost sacred place in my mind and although I have been sadly disillusioned, I am still slightly shocked at some of the things I see women do and hear said about them.

In those days white women never entered my mind as a thing to be possessed. They were beautiful and elegant to look at but I never longed for or desired one. I was too occupied feeling my own importance.

I frankly admit that white women seem to be particularly fascinating for most Negro men. It has always been a strange thing to me, and now after having associated with white women for five years or so, it seems very extraordinary.

It is not that white women are not nice, because they are and exceptionally so. They are charming and very considerate. But even though I am here in Europe and far removed from the prejudices and taboos of America, I still have a distrust of white women that was driven into my very soul on so many occasions by knowing Negro men who have suffered terrible deaths because they allowed themselves to be enticed by white women.

Such incidents as those have always made me wary of white women. I did not trust them. I brought this feeling to Europe with me. When I met Nancy Cunard I viewed her with great suspicion and distrust.

My suspicions of Nancy—because she is white—from the beginning were only intensified when I learned she was rather free with her affections (and I found that out in Venice).

All of that served as an immediate check on any outflow of feelings that might have been let loose.

Yet, I greatly admired her flashes of intelligence, and once thought that I might make some real progress by associating with her. So I overlooked a great many things after the beginning because my heart was never at stake. I imagined that I might carve a successful future out of the situation. I was elated when she showed interest in the Negro question and hoped for some real results. I gladly consented to give her the names of all the American Negroes of note that I thought would be of use to her in increasing her knowledge of Negro affairs and achievements. At that time I hoped she would do something for my race.

But those hopes, like all of the rest I possessed, were smothered and shattered. In the maelstrom of changes in which I found myself, more than once I tried to reach the edge of its swirling events. But each attempt failed and I always discovered that instead of reaching the calm I so desired I was again being carried along by the momentum of the whirling waters in which I had willingly stepped.

For the woman herself, I know of no better example who is so ruled by whims and changes. She exemplified this in her rapid change of lovers and her hot and then cooling attachment to any passing desire. She could stay nowhere for any extended period unless she was so busy she could not take in her environment and once she did that she immediately tired of it.

The craze to run a private printing press lasted until it interfered with her pleasure. The film "L'Age d'Or" came next. Then the Negro anthology and now I understand she is writing a scenario for a great Negro film to be done sometime in the future—where and how to be decided later.

This instability in Nancy's character I think is her greatest fault. I was never certain what she would do next. She left me flatly stranded on two occasions and almost did so on another.

She could be called almost heartless in her relations with

those who professed to love her. I really believe she derived a great deal of personal satisfaction in hearing some man threaten to commit suicide because of her. I always told her I would not prick my finger with a pin over any woman. And when she cast some lover aside he became as dirt under her feet. Any additional protestations of love only aroused laughter and contempt in her.

Born an aristocrat, her early training was of the nature to enable her to fill a position in the highest social circles of England. The influence of her birth and the manner in which she passed her childhood and early womanhood left a lasting impression on her character. She was always the dominant spirit in whatever group she moved and all and sundry paid her homage.

Now as my mind runs over the people I have met through her I realize that practically all of them were literary people, musicians or painters. With but few exceptions most of them were what is sometimes styled as queer. There are some notable exceptions however. I met Wyndham Lewis, who, I was told, was considered one of the greatest literary geniuses in England. Nancy escorted me to his small and unpretentious rooms "somewhere in London" and we talked pleasantly while consuming drinks.

I formed no special opinion of him aside from the fact that I thought him a rather intense and reticent individual. It was said that he was a very difficult person with whom to get an audience. However, he was pleasant enough to me.

I have an idea that most of these people that I met through Nancy probably disapproved of her manner in showing her lack of a racial or color feeling. It is significant that as the years passed she saw less and less of the people she saw when I first met her.

But in this as in all else, she could see nothing but her own viewpoint, and to her that was all self-sufficient. So as she grew bolder and more demonstrative with her Negro friends her more conservative white friends fell away. Not that I think they were prejudiced against Negroes but they did not feel it necessary to go to the extremes to which Nancy went.

In a way, Nancy was very liberal. She rarely passed a poor beggar without giving something. She would respond quickly to pleas of distress. She refused to kill any living thing. She once stopped me from killing a snake in the road that led to the house in the country. Nevertheless, she handled the feelings of human beings very carelessly indeed. The most glaring example of this I have saved until the last. It was when she met Edward Cummings, the American author who wrote *The Enormous Room*. Cummings had come to Paris with his wife.

Nancy had always expressed a great admiration for Cummings' works and often said she would be delighted to meet him. When he arrived he was much in the company of Eugene MacCown.

One night when Nancy was away I bumped into Eugene and Cummings who was with his wife in Montparnasse. We formed a party and, after several drinks, taxied over to finish the evening in Montmartre.

When Nancy returned I informed her that I had met Cummings. She immediately indicated her desire to meet him and through Eugene a meeting was arranged at a café in Montmartre.

Eugene, Cummings and his wife and I arrived punctually. We ordered drinks and expectantly waited for Nancy. As always she was late, very late. She finally arrived—blind drunk. She staggered to the table with a very vacant expression on her face and practically fell into a chair.

"Nancy, this is Mr. and Mrs. Cummings," said Eugene.

Then a most amazing thing happened. Without a preliminary word, without acknowledging the introduction, Nancy fixed a most contemptuous stare at Cummings and in the most unpleasant tones imaginable said:

"Oh, so you are Cummings eh?"

He replied in the affirmative. She continued:

"Well, I can't imagine anyone that looks like you writing

a book like *The Enormous Room*. I am disappointed in your appearance. How did you do it?"

Her words fell like a bombshell. Eugene tried to remonstrate with her but of no avail. She again addressed herself directly to Cummings and said some terrible things. She ignored Mrs. Cummings entirely. No completely insane person could have conducted themselves any worse. She heaped abuse on Cummings so rapidly that, coupled with our astonishment, we sat tongue-tied.

At the first break in her tirade, Cummings very quietly stated that since that was her opinion of him, he did not see the need of prolonging his stay in her company. He quietly left with his wife.

Eugene's feelings were outraged and I was downright mad, through and through. I had never heard of and certainly never witnessed before such a colossal display of rudeness and bad manners. Eugene expressed his thoughts briefly and went away, leaving me with Nancy.

I told her what a drunken fool she was and suggested that she go to her hotel immediately. She agreed to go on the condition that I go to the Costa Bar with her first. I consented but had reason to regret my decision.

On the way to the bar in a taxi I asked her why she did such an awful thing. Her replies were most unintelligible but I managed to understand a phrase or so.

"He is the kind who would say NIGGER; I don't like his face," she mumbled.

We arrived at the Costa Bar, which, at that time, was always filled with colored people, mostly Americans. We took a table and ordered drinks. She kept repeating "he is the kind who would say nigger" and loudly accentuating the word "nigger." Very naturally all of the Negroes in the place became all attention when the word was spoken and looked to see where it came from.

Unfortunately for me I was the only person in the place who knew what it was all about. All that they heard was the word nigger. They promptly came to the conclusion that

Nancy was calling me a nigger. I had a devil of a time explaining why I had sat quietly and let a white woman call me a nigger and in public at that.

On the other hand she could be sweet to a person on sight and tell them all sorts of encouraging things. She could make almost anyone believe that she would give them material assistance and then become greatly annoyed when asked for help. If they persisted they were rudely turned away.

She has often told me that she had never met a colored man who did not want money. I tried to explain to her that when a white woman became intimate with a colored man he usually expected to get money from her. My words never deterred her, however, in her quest of more Negro friends.

I have spoken of Nancy's great effort, the Negro anthology, and I wish to add that this book caused her name to go to the four corners of the earth. Black people have hailed her and the book. A Negro school in Africa has been named for her. The book has been banned in one or two colonies.

Again, I must give credit for the great energy put forth to collect such a work. It was dedicated to me but I frankly think that on the whole the book is a failure. It records much that could have better remained unrecorded. She also gives the book an unmistakably communistic flavor, which, for the most part, is her own doing. She prefaces the book by trying to convey the theory that the Soviet form of government offers the only hope for the Negro. I don't think that is true at all and I am sure there are thousands of black men who think as I.

Then too, I do not believe that Nancy had the background that a person who attempts to do a great work for a whole race should possess. The book is shallow and empty. It makes a lot of noise, but like a big drum it has little inside.

Time was hanging heavy on Nancy's hands then. She had nothing to do. The idea came and probably without taking into consideration the importance of the task, ignoring her lack of preparation or knowledge of the question, she dived into the mammoth job and only came out by sheer endurance. I certainly admire her nerve but have little respect for her good judgement.

I often told Nancy that being in the limelight of the public placed responsibilities upon her. My argument was that persons who have reached the heights of success were not any longer the sole directors of their actions. I argued that her name coupled with all of the notoriety brought about by the book made a heroine of her in the eyes of thousands of Negroes. She was a champion of the black man's rights and should therefore try to live up to that standard.

She pooh-poohed the idea, and told me everyone has the right to live as they choose. Some day this may become a fact but I am firmly of the opinion that when we reach a position where our personal desires or actions reflect to the detriment of others that the good of the many should become paramount.

I believe that people should be left to choose their companions socially without interference from any source. But as long as we live in communities, just so long shall we have to practice restraint as to our actions and conduct. This is applicable to races and especially so to Negroes who come in contact with white people in Europe and America.

Some white people dislike Negroes but they really don't know why. Some are prejudiced and can't explain their prejudices. A white man in London once told me that he had no prejudice against Negroes but somehow he had a queer feeling when he saw a Negro man dancing with a white woman. I asked him how he felt when the position was reversed. He admitted he did not have the same sort of feeling.

It is a generally accepted theory among Negro men that white women consider them as having superior sexual powers to those of white men. This belief has persisted until now black men feel that it is an established fact. I am sure a great many white women must think this is true, especially in Europe.

In the case of Nancy I am not at all certain of her ideas about this particular point. People are so different and Nancy is a most extraordinary person. She has no bridle to her desire. She goes from one to another with evident pleasure. The satisfaction of the senses is evidently the driving force. But:

"Fools rush in where angels fear to tread" and "he who dances must pay the piper." Poor Nancy has paid and is paying now for the rushing in and dancing she has done in the past.

A very pitiful scene occurred between us towards the end of our associations. We had one of our frequently recurring quarrels one morning. After having my say I went to my room and to bed. She came to my door and revived the argument. To stop it all I got up and dressed and proposed to leave for good. She remarked:

"Oh, you're just like all the rest. The old girl (meaning herself) is broke now. Got no money. You're like all other rats, leaving a sinking ship."

I pitied her then. I wondered if she ever thought of the times when she could have made real true friends but had let her own personal desires ignore the chances.

Many hours have I pondered over the reason why Nancy wanted me around her. She once told me that I was the only person who never bored her. Yet, she would quarrel with me over the smallest things. She would send for me from most anywhere but soon after my arrival she would be telling me she could not pay my keep.

Then why send for me? Why would she always withdraw her assistance at the very moment I needed it most? It was more than I could ever understand.

There are many things about Nancy I could never understand. I have read several books about famous and notorious women but I honestly believe Nancy Cunard oddly stands out as a unique character among women of all time. It is hard to say in what peculiar niche she would best fit.

She was born to the purple but has thrown it all aside. Now she finds herself in a new and hostile environment, among enemies about whom she knows nothing and can never understand. She has tried to break down impregnable barriers with foolish and futile weapons; she has tried to dip an ocean dry with a spoon.

She seems to have forgotten that instead of raising the lowest of the black race to her level by associating with them she lowers herself to their level. Every extreme has a mean and every mean has an extreme. She knows only extremes.

Equality in relations between black and white races is a condition that is most desired but in reaching that goal the method of approach should be decent and rational. That is not the method she has adopted. I don't think she will ever understand the real feelings most Negro men possess towards white women.

Regretfully, black men are seemingly irresistibly attracted by white women. And because of that many black men make the most complete fools of themselves over what is practically the dregs of humanity and proudly disport themselves with nothing more than whores—as long as they are white.

Again, American Negroes feel that white women live in mortal terror of their men and dare not confess to a willful violation of the moral code established for them. So the black man secretly gets satisfaction in telling himself that the white woman desires him and is only awaiting her opportunity to associate with him.

I don't believe any such rot as this. In fact, any black man or woman who places absolute confidence in the personal love and affection of a white person appears to me as a plain fool. My mind can conceive of circumstances and conditions in which I would be very skeptical of the fidelity of a white woman to a Negro man and I have no faith whatever in the love of a white man for a Negro woman. He very plainly evinces the fact that he only wants a Negro woman for his selfish and secret pleasure.

There are, I suppose, exceptions to the rule, but I have never witnessed one in my life where Americans are concerned.

Some Negroes have been senseless enough to marry white women in Europe and take them back to America with them. The usual fate awaits them. The whites won't accept them and the Negroes insult them. There are instances of marriages between white men and Negro women in Europe but I know of very few and I know of no white man with the temerity to take a black wife back to America with him. I have thought of all this and have wondered why any Negro with brains would allow himself to become thoroughly infatuated with a white woman.

I no longer hate white people as a whole. In fact, I have learned that some white people are my very best friends. I have learned that a white man is of infinitely more use to me than any black man who in reality professes to be a friend. I honestly believe that the average white man in Europe or America is to be more trusted and depended upon in his dealings with black people than black people among themselves.

I believe there are many white Americans who would gladly drop all pretense of color prejudices even in America were they permitted to do so. I believe the younger generation of white people are more sensible about the race question than those that have passed.

My experiences have taught me many lessons regarding race relations, especially in Europe. But in spite of the many encouraging aspects of conditions in Europe, in spite of the absence of prejudice as it exists in America, I am absolutely convinced that the greatest happiness and contentment for black people is to be found among themselves. And regardless of how many taboos and restrictions are dropped I still feel that there will always be a definite blood pull among Negroes themselves.

Practically all of my time in Europe has been spent with white people. I doubt if any American black man in recent years has lived such a full life among white people as I. However, after months of separation from colored people I found myself tiring of seeing white faces and my heart would leap with joy on seeing one of my own race. This is a very natural reaction I should think with any race.

Still, I don't think that most of the people I have met in

Europe have considered the color of my skin excepting that it was in my favor. In fact, they have probably been much nicer to me than most Negroes would have been to me.

I have enjoyed myself immensely. I have learned a lot. I now look on life from a different slant. From hate, my feelings toward white people have become tolerant. I know that all white people do not hate Negroes.

Yet, I followed the rainbow of a white woman's attractions and found at the end only disillusionment and disappointment. I have no regrets, however, except that I let so many precious years go by that could have meant so much to me professionally.

That I did not take heed and conduct my life according to sane reasoning when I found where the end of the curious relation I started was going to lead I can only lay to circumstance and the strange attraction she held for me. Nancy and I were like oil and water. There was no possibility of mixing.

In the end, I am forced to wonder if there are any genuinely contented mixed couples. This desired state is rare enough among people of the same blood and I am forced to the conclusion that it is rarer still among people so different as whites and blacks.

This is not a plea for segregation of the races though on account of color or anything else. But it is a distinct warning to black men to be cautious as to how they let their feelings go in regard to white women and, above all, never dream of sacrificing the chance of a career by following the flash of a woman's fancy and especially that of a white woman.

For me, that is all over. I have returned to my own. I am content.

EPILOGUE

Epilogue

by Robert L. Allen

HENRY CROWDER did not immediately return to his own, if by that is meant his wife in the United States. He stayed in Europe, keeping himself going by taking occasional jobs, until World War II.

In Paris Crowder met a white American journalist by the name of Hugo Speck. Speck had worked for the *Chicago Tribune* before coming to London in 1931 to join the International News Service. In 1934 he moved to Paris to work for the Universal News Service. He was also the Paris correspondent for *Variety*. Exactly when Crowder met Speck (who is possibly the unnamed "staunch white man friend" Crowder refers to toward the end of his text) is unknown. What is known is that on May 14, 1935, just weeks after Nancy and Henry had broken up, Speck and Crowder signed an agreement proposing a collaboration in doing a book or articles "based on Henry Crowder's experiences with, and views of, his life with Nancy Cunard."

The agreement stipulated that Crowder would supply the facts, and assume full responsibility for their truthfulness and any legal action that might ensue from publication of the book. Speck would "lend all possible aid in editing and preparing for publication such book . . . including efforts to secure [a] suitable publisher." They agreed to split the royalties 50-50. Speck further agreed to "lend such financial aid to Henry Crowder as may be reasonably possible until the completion of such book . . ., it being understood and agreed that any such sums advanced to Henry Crowder by Hugo

Speck shall be considered a loan and shall be repayable not later than the date payment is received for such book . . ." How much Speck advanced to Crowder is not known. The agreement was duly witnessed and signed by both men.

The manuscript they prepared was not published. Hugo's brother, Ernest, recently retired from Sul Ross State University in Texas where he was a professor of English, speculates that they did not try to find a publisher because it was assumed that Lady Cunard, then still alive, would block publication. The manuscript came into the possession of Ernest Speck after Hugo's death in 1970. I learned of its existence from references in Anne Chisholm's 1979 biography of Nancy.

Nancy and Henry never saw each other again. After he returned to Washington they corresponded occasionally. He found a job in the U.S. Customs Bureau and settled down to a conventional life. In one letter written in 1953 he commented: "Life for me here in the USA is now following a set pattern. Pretty dull and monotonous but I am living and going through the motions of life without any special interest. . . ." In 1954 she apparently sent him a copy of her book on Norman Douglas. He wrote back in November to thank her. "I have read the book entirely and find it very interesting and informative," he commented. As for his own life, he wrote: "I am a clerk. I handle all outgoing mail of the Coast Guard headquarters. The job is pleasant and the hours of work agreeable . . ." He said that his music had improved and that he was devoting a great deal of time to the piano and singing. Although he said nothing about his personal life, he was obviously living a life very different from the old days with Nancy. "As for nightclubs—all that is a thing of the past— never cared much for them anyway." Somewhat wistfully he wrote: "I am not happy, and I am not sad."

The one thing that did appear to excite Crowder was the changing racial situation in the U.S. In May 1954 the Supreme Court had decreed that segregation in the public schools was unconstitutional. "Things are changing rapidly here in America along the color line," he wrote. "Great and fundamental changes." He mentioned desegregation efforts in the schools, the military, restaurants and theaters. "A lot remains to be done," he added, "but we are grateful . . . Still, I would love to see Europe again."

His wish to see Europe again was not to be granted. Nancy asked an American friend, Charles Burkhart, to look up Crowder. In early 1955 Burkhart learned that Crowder, who would have been about 60 years old, had died. Burkhart wrote Nancy to give her this news. On April 24 she replied to his letter.

> And so Henry is dead—
> How extraordinary it is to me to think of the way this news comes to me . . . Do you know that, otherwise, I should *never* have known? Is this what happens when one asks a friend to look for the long-dead past? Pretty obviously, I should never have seen him again. He might have been dead from 1935 to 1947, for all I knew. Henry made me—and so be it . . . Others have loved me more (?), and I, perhaps, others. No probably not, for me, has this been true. In any case: Henry made me. I thank him.

Later Nancy received a letter from Henry Crowder's wife saying that she, the wife, was Crowder's only true, loving wife. The two women had never met, and, as far as is known, this was the only communication between them.

After the publication of *Negro* in 1934 Nancy's life continued with its characteristic intensity. She flung herself into the republican cause during the Spanish civil war. She went to Spain, wrote impassioned articles, and, in the closing moments of the war, rescued five men from Spanish refugee camps, taking them to her house at Réanville.

Interestingly, many of her news dispatches were written for the Associated Negro Press, a news agency based in Chicago that served black newspapers in the U.S. She had been appointed one of their correspondents during the Abyssinian crisis and she wrote articles fervently in favor of Haile Selassie whom she portrayed as progressive African leader being hounded by the imperialist Italian fascists. For the next twenty years or so she would write regularly for the ANP from Europe and England and during visits to South America and the Caribbean.

Despite her involvement in other causes, Nancy's commitment to racial equality remained undiminished during the rest of her life. In 1943 she and George Padmore, a leftist black political activist, published a pamphlet, entitled *The White Man's Duty,* that discussed how the war should affect the attitude of Britain towards race prejudice at home and the aspirations of the colonies for self-government. They called for an act of parliament to ban racial discrimination and make possible "equal opportunities . . . in all fields of life." They also advocated immediate self-government and nationalization of the economies of the colonies, with them being federated into "a Socialist Commonwealth." The pamphlet, according to Nancy, sold nearly 20,000 copies.

Nancy maintained links with the Colonial Centre in London, the Negro Welfare Centre in Liverpool, and the West African Students Union, where she was a frequent visitor. When she learned of incidents of racial discrimination she turned to her trusty typewriter and fired off a letter of protest.

She herself summed up the place of the struggle for racial equality in her life. In 1956, while mulling over the possibility of writing an autobiography, she outlined some major themes in her private notebook.

When of SELF writing: Re the three main things.

1. Equality of races.
2. Of sexes.
3. Of classes.

I am in accord with all countries and individuals who feel, and act, as I do on this score.

Toward the end of her life Nancy Cunard was afflicted with debilitating, painful illness, made worse by her continued heavy drinking. Yet, until the end she was on the move, returning to France from England in the last year of her life. (Her house at Chapelle-Réanville had been sacked by the Germans during the war.) A week after her 70th birthday, on March 16, 1965, in the public ward of a French hospital, she died. Three days before her death she told her nurses that she was working on a long poem against all wars.

The relationship between Henry Crowder and Nancy Cunard was like a minefield filled with psychological booby-traps. That they survived it is a miracle; that they were both battered and bruised is not surprising. They could hardly have known what they were getting into when they met. Both were looking for *something* but what they found was completely unexpected. In a curious dance, reminiscent of Nancy's African dreams, they oscillated around each other for almost seven years. Clearly there was something that each found powerfully attractive in the other, but there were also many moments of antipathy.

Matters were not made easier by the overt and subtle racist hostility they encountered. The vilifications in the press, the hate mail, the taunts on the streets, these they could have anticipated. More difficult to deal with were the reactions of friends. Nancy was bitterly disappointed when George Moore, her "first friend" and a proponent of free thought and anti-bigotry, or so she thought, admitted that he could not "get on with a black man or a brown man." They must have also sensed the patronizing attitude of friends who might smile when they met but then made racist remarks behind their backs or in private letters and journals. Richard Aldington, who professed to like Henry, commonly referred to blacks, including Crowder, as "niggers" in his letters. In his view Henry was only a "sexual drug" on which Nancy was hooked. To Brian Howard, writing in his journal, Henry was "impassive, infinitely patient, stupid." To others Henry was a "simple soul" incapable of appreciating the difference between African art and rococo Italian tables.

Henry, sensing that he was in a delicate position being

publicly on intimate terms with a wealthy white woman, even if it was in Europe, adopted an inoffensive amiability as a kind of defensive covering. He could sing spirituals with Ezra Pound and chat genially with others he must have suspected secretly despised him. This was quite different from the brash young Crowder depicted in his *Negro* essay, a man who fought racist thugs on the streets. But in America there were other blacks to come to his aid; in Europe and England he knew he was alone.

As for Nancy, her style was always confrontational, sometimes hysterical as in the encounter with the American poet Edward Cummings (e.e. cummings) described by Crowder. She would have agreed with military strategists who argue that the best defense is an attack. She was always a fighter; accommodation was beyond her comprehension.

Though each developed a characteristic style of coping with racism its poison slipped insidiously into their relationship and their perceptions of each other. Nancy sometimes seems to have felt that Henry was not quite exotic enough— she wished he were blacker and more "African." "Be more *African,* be more *African,*" she once urged him. "But I ain't African. I'm *American,*" was his reply. Henry, seeing Nancy through a lens colored by racism and sexism, hoped to "carve a successful future" out of his relationship with this wealthy white woman. "When a white woman became intimate with a colored man," he once told Nancy, "he usually expected to get money from her." Henry did not exempt himself from this expectation.

Nancy could not escape her racial and class background and this manifested itself in her treatment of Henry. On more than one occasion she treated him contemptuously, as though he were her servant. And she could be physically abusive when she had been drinking. A mutual friend, Janet Flanner, recalled seeing Crowder one day with a set of bruise marks. She asked him what happened. "Just braceletwork, Miss Janet," he replied sardonically.

Neither was Crowder free of the stamp of being educated in socially conscious black Atlanta. He did not like Nancy's lower-class black friends, and he avoided associating with them. In a comment worthy of Lady Cunard he could not resist pointing out that Nancy "seems to have forgotten that instead of raising the lowest of the black race to her level by associating with them she lowers herself to their level." He disliked, and sometimes ridiculed, many of the blacks he met in Europe, including the mysterious "Rogers" who may have been the famous black journalist (and later historian) J.A. Rogers. Carrying his self-hating assessment even further Crowder concluded: "I have learned that a white man is of infinitely more use to me than any black man who in reality professes to be a friend. I honestly believe that the average white man in Europe or America is more to be trusted and depended upon in his dealings with black people than black people among themselves."

Although bemoaning the perils of involvements with white women, Crowder hardly hesitated when Nancy Cunard offered him her hospitality. In very short order he also came to enjoy the pleasures of her body and the comforts provided by her pocketbook. Yet he complains that she did not do more for him and that she was niggling in doling out money to him. Nancy was certainly erratic in her dealings with money, perhaps because she could never be certain that her mother would not cut her off completely. Still it is clear that over the years of their relationship she at times supported Crowder financially, helped him with his music (paying for lessons and instruments, publishing his work), bought him a car, enabled him to travel and make contacts, and literally saved him when he was down and out in Depression-era Washington. If Crowder failed to convert this assistance into greater personal success he must bear at least part of the responsibility himself.

Henry Crowder depicts himself as the injured party in his relationship with Nancy Cunard. One wonders how his wife and son felt. In 1916 he had fathered a son, Henry, Jr., but he never mentions this son nor hints of having any thoughts of him. For a time after he arrived in Europe he sent money to his wife, but this was discontinued and she was left to fend for herself. To be sure, he was estranged from his wife, but not so much that he could not return to her after he left Nancy.

If Nancy was flawed, Henry was no gem. What was it, finally, that they saw in each other, that each apparently found so irresistible? Did they love each other, or was their relationship simply an instance of mutual use and abuse? I believe that they did love each other—but there were also powerful unconscious forces drawing them together, forces that would eventually drive them apart.

Nancy freely admitted that she loved Henry. In Henry she found a measure of emotional stability and a comforting companionship that were nourishing and calming in her hectic life. She loved to listen to him playing the piano as she worked at the press in Réanville. He was her sturdy "tree." She was also fascinated, at least at first, by the life he lived as a musician, by the life he lived as a black man in America, by who he was. He never bored her. Henry was the living personification of her love affair with black culture.

At the same time he was like her house at Chapelle-Réanville—though she loved him she must always leave him to seek other adventures. Neither she nor Henry had much to say about their sex life. Its importance faded with time; each found other lovers. Like some women who have been sexually abused in childhood, Nancy was promiscuous while also experiencing difficulty in being sexually satisfied. She was sexually adventurous while also being conventional, even inhibited. She could have many lovers at once, but might find one man too demanding. In any case, it was not sex that bound Nancy and Henry together.

It was Nancy's tragedy that she felt driven to flee her past without ever understanding it. In a memoir Raymond Michelet recalled that "Nancy forged ahead, fleeing from something, never stopping to consider, never turning back, burning everything behind her, things she had loved, people she might have loved . . ." What was she fleeing? Michelet could not say. A clue is provided by her resistance to writing an autobiography, though urged by editors and friends. She scribbled some notes toward an autobiography but concluded, "I do not want to write this book." She did not like to look back; an autobiography would have demanded reflection on her past and this she apparently did not wish to do. But without understanding her past she could not be fully at ease in the present and consequently she was always compelled to dash madly into the future.

Perhaps Nancy could not bear the thought of how much she might resemble her mother, Lady Cunard. Both were striving to make a mark in the worlds they deemed important: Lady Cunard as a London hostess, Nancy in *belles lettres*. Both had complex multiple relationships with men that were sometimes painful to others and disruptive of domestic tranquility. Both could be arrogant and demanding. Both were accused of being coldly sensual and unloving. To look objectively at her mother might result in seeing unpleasant things about herself; it might fracture her self-image. This Nancy could not bear; better to throw brickbats and run.

Henry was infatuated with Nancy, but early in their relationship, he claimed, any love he may have felt for her was killed; still, a mysteriously compelling force kept him with her. Time and time again this strange force brought him back to her. To be sure, money played its part in the story but there was more that attracted him to her. Nancy lived with an intense vitality that was captivating; several writers who knew her have commented on this quality. I believe this was what drew Crowder to her—her passionate interests, her independence of thought, her wilfulness, her love of travel, her commitment to things beyond herself, even her wild emotional swings. This was the "indescribable force" that bound him to her. She was a force, an emotional and intellectual magnet he could not resist. Where he pictured himself as cool, aloof, detached, she was always passionately engaged, and this attracted him. Where he floated with the current she swam against it and created a vortex that pulled him along, introducing him to new adventures that were always fascinating, never dull.

Crowder could not name the "invisible" power that bound him to Nancy, perhaps because to do so would mean becoming conscious of his own emotional void, the lack of deep feeling that had characterized most of his adult life. Even his music, except when he could get away to the country, seemed more of a job or business than a passion. Behind his amiability, behind his self-righteousness I think there was concealed a repressed, controlled personality that yearned for the emotional expressiveness Nancy personified. Henry's major childhood memories are of the strict and pious upbringing imposed by his father. Although he was the baby of the family he received little loving tenderness. An emotional, sensitive child, he could not bear to hurt the feelings of others nor witness the slaughter of farm animals. Seeking to please his parents, little Henry learned to control his emotions and "tried to be goodness itself." A "goody good" boy, he gloried in hearing his "mother tell friends or neighbors what a perfect child was Henry." But perfection was not long to be his. "Fanatically religious" though he was, the "devil" introduced him to sexual desire, much to his discomfiture. He agonized with feelings of guilt and resolved not to engage in "shady affairs" like other boys he knew. He struggled mightily, though not always successfully, "to gain control over this passion." It would take years for him to finally renounce the "hypocrisy of religion," and he never completely freed himself of the learned, but unconscious, need to hold his emotions in check.

Sadly, Crowder could not admit his emotional neediness; indeed he denied it and thus was compelled to portray Nancy as the evil white bitch, motivated only by her own selfish pleasure and gratification. Her spontaneity, her genuine generosity toward him and others, her sincere commitment to people and causes all vanished behind the cloud of his denial. Obscured also was the emotional bonding between them that nourished the growth of both of them. This was Henry Crowder's tragedy—that in the end he must turn against the very qualities in Nancy Cunard that he loved, which were the things in himself he suppressed.

SOURCES CONSULTED

Chisholm, Anne, *Nancy Cunard*. Penguin Books, 1980.

Cunard, Nancy (ed.), *Negro: An Anthology*. Abridged edition by Hugh Ford. Frederick Ungar Publishing Co., 1970.

Cunard, Nancy, *These Were the Hours*. Edited by Hugh Ford. Southern Illinois University Press, 1969.

Ford, Hugh (ed.), *Nancy Cunard: Brave Poet, Indomitable Rebel, 1896–1965*. Chilton Book Company, 1968.

Speck, Ernest B., "Henry Crowder: Nancy Cunard's 'Tree,'" in *Lost Generation Journal*. Vol. VI, Number 1, Summer 1979.